Nancy Kominsky

PASTEL & OIL PAINTING

This edition published 1995 by Diamond Books
77-85 Fulham Palace Road
Hammersmith, London W6 8JB

First published in two volumes:

Painting with Pastels © Nancy Kominsky 1986
First published in the US in 1990 by HarperCollins Books
First published in the UK in Lions in 1992

Reading the letter by Edgar Degas c. 1884 courtesy of
The Burrell Collection – Glasgow Museums and Art Galleries

Oil Painting for the Beginner © Nancy Kominsky 1982
First published in 1982 by HarperCollins*Publishers*
Designed and produced by The Rainbird
Publishing Group Ltd

Printed in Italy

ISBN 0 261 66465 4

Contents

PAINTING WITH PASTELS

PAINTING IN OILS

PAINTING WITH PASTELS

Nancy Kominsky

Nancy Kominsky, a native Philadelphian, is a portrait painter, international lecturer, teacher and author, who now lives in Rome. She studied at the Graphic Sketch Club, Philadelphia, Pa. Cooper Union, New York City and under Theodore Lukits, a well-known portrait painter, in California. She worked for three years painting and sculpturing on scaled dioramas for a Pennsylvania Museum.

In 1963, faced with the prospect of no income and at the urging of a friend, she opened her first Sunday Painters Art Studio in Burbank, California. She devised a unique 'anyone can paint' system of teaching which became instantly successful.

In 1966 she moved to Rome and opened the equally successful Sunday Painters of Rome Studio, teaching personnel from many embassies of the world there how to paint. She has completed four highly acclaimed networked television series of thirteen programmes each and twenty-six programmes in the United States. Her television series is currently being broadcast in places as far afield as Malaysia, Iceland and the United Arab Emirates. She has also written many very successful painting books which have been translated into several languages.

Foreword

When I first became interested in art, at a very tender age, I naturally started drawing with a pencil. Later, when I attended art school, I graduated to charcoal. Some students branched off into watercolours and oils but I started to use a set of pastels which I had received as a gift. My interest grew after having seen the marvellous pastel paintings of the famous Impressionist, Edgar Degas, such as *Reading the letter* (overleaf).

Recently I discovered an old pastel portrait of my husband's grandmother which had been painted in 1898. To my utter amazement fine sandpaper had been used as the background material. It was in a dreadful condition but I managed to restore it, with oil pastels instead of the soft chalk pastels of the original. I then decided to use the technique of oil pastels on sandpaper as the basis for a new book, incorporating the same simple step-by-step method which had been so successful in my books and television programmes about oil painting. This system, which has specific instructions, uses oil pastels, sandpaper and coloured paper and will help you produce, at the very first attempt, exciting and vibrant paintings.

Oil pastels have the brilliance of oil paints whereas soft chalk pastels tend to be tints of colour and rather difficult to use. Unlike oil paints, however, oil pastels do not require mixing and, unlike soft chalk pastels, they do not need any fixative. Oil pastels are a very clean and quick medium to work in – you can paint at anytime, anywhere and don't have to wait for your painting to dry! They are also very cheap; the outlay for all the materials is relatively little, which is practical for those with limited funds. You don't need lots of space either!

Painting with oil pastels is not difficult – it is simply a question of learning the best technique. With my straightforward system you will face a new and exciting challenge and will, I promise, be thrilled with the results.

Nancy Kominsky

Reading the letter by Edgar Degas c. 1884

Before you paint

MAKES OF PASTEL

Read these notes carefully before starting to paint.

You can use any make of oil pastel for these pictures – a few examples are Sakura Cray-pas, Guitar and Contélor. However, make sure you don't buy the soft chalk pastels which are softer in colour and texture and which require a different painting technique. In the text I have used the most common names for each colour, e.g. Yellow Ochre or Cobalt Blue, but don't worry if your pastels have different names or even slightly different shades of the colours. Because my step-by-step method is based on tonal values, i.e. light, medium and dark shades, it will not matter if the shades themselves vary slightly from the ones in the book. All that matters is that you have the tonal values required for each stage of a painting. For example, to paint a particular object, the light tone might be Yellow Green, the medium tone Green and the dark tone Deep Green. Each of the tonal values – light, medium and dark (and extra light if necessary) – are indicated by colour swatches at the beginning of each section. If you are at all unsure of which colours to use, simply find the nearest colour match by using the shade card on this page – any differences in colour won't affect your painting.

HOW MANY TO BUY

Most pastels come in boxes of 12, 24-25, and 36-40. You should buy the medium-sized box with 24-25 colours. You can buy single colours to replace any you use up, but if you are going to attempt all the paintings in the book you may find it cheaper in the long run to buy an extra box of 12 pastels which will contain all the main colours.

THE PAINTINGS

The painting projects in this book have been carefully planned to help you develop your painting skills progressively. Florals, as in the first project, *Mixed Bouquet*, are generally the easiest to begin with. As you become more experienced and familiar with your materials, and with my simplified step-by-step technique, you will be able to handle the more ambitious projects later in the book. Just keep painting!

PAINTING TECHNIQUE

The pastel should be held lightly while stroking on the colour. Do not press hard unless this is specified in the instructions. The sandpaper should not be filled in with solid colour unless indicated. In most cases the sandpaper should show through the colour. Other colours can then be blended in or added on top. This is not only an interesting effect but saves pastels! In creating form your strokes are important. For example, use round strokes for round objects. Don't panic when colouring, just paint slowly and your pictures will look lovely.

As a general rule, paint in the dark tones first, followed by the middle tones and then the light tones. Only mix tones where they meet so as not to lose tonal values or muddy the colours. This is very important to preserve the contrast between light and dark in the paintings.

WORKING WITH PASTELS

As you work you will have to remove bits of the paper label. When this happens make sure you match your pastels with the colour swatches for each painting project. It is best to take the pastels out of their box and line them up alongside your painting area. Keep them in one place – this will save both time and frustration!

SHADOWS

You will see that all the paintings take account of the shadows which are formed by light shining on one side of an object. If light is shining on the left of an object, the shadow will fall on the right. If the light is shining on the right, the shadow will fall on the left. Paint the shadows in lightly at first – you can always darken them later.

MOUNTING YOUR PICTURES

Your pictures will look much more professional, and larger, if you mount them. One of the easiest ways is to use coloured paper – any sort will do, but if it is slightly stiff it will provide some support for your painting. Choose a colour that will tone with the painting, for example, brown for *First Snow* or yellow for *Fruit and Flowers*. The mounting paper should ideally be about 8cm (3in) larger all round than your painting. Place the painting in the centre and mark the corners lightly on the mounting paper. Using a little clear glue; carefully stick down the painting using the pencil marks as guidelines. Don't use too much glue as it might soak through the paper and spoil your painting. You can, if you wish, then frame your picture under glass. You can buy simple picture frames quite inexpensively from stores and art shops.

PAINTING MATERIALS

The following is a list of pastels and other painting materials required for the eleven paintings in the book.

1. Pastels
(a) One set of 24-25 oil pastels.
(b) Two extra sticks of white oil pastel.

2. Pencils
(a) Two HB lead pencils.
(b) One thin or medium charcoal pencil.
(c) One purple pastel pencil (Contélor Number 5).

3. Double pencil sharpener

4. Erasers
Two kneadable putty erasers for erasing grids etc.

5. Drawing paper
To paint all the pictures in this book you will need nine pieces of medium fine sandpaper and two pieces of coloured paper. They can be any size but I used, and can recommend: eight pieces of medium fine sandpaper 23×30cm (9×12in) and one piece of medium fine sandpaper 30×35cm (12×14in). You can buy very large pieces of sandpaper and cut them to size. Painting on sandpaper gives an exciting texture but you can, if you wish, paint on sugar paper (construction paper). You will also need two pieces of light blue paper 23×30cm (9×12in). You can use blue sugar (construction) paper or Ingres drawing paper which is widely available.

6. Mounting paper
See the note on mounting your pictures on page10.

7. Easel
Use whatever is available, but I think a table easel is best. Not only does it fold away, but the table on which you place the easel provides a good surface to hold your painting equipment (see illustration).

8. Drawing board
This is to place on your easel to support your paintings. You don't have to buy one especially but can use any available stiff cardboard. Make sure it is larger than your painting.

9. Work area
You can use any space available. Pastel painting requires very little space for preparation and cleaning up.

10. Scrap paper
Two extra pieces of sandpaper – any size. These are to clean the pastels before going from one colour to another. Scrape the tip of the pastel, and the sides if necessary, lightly in a circular motion on the sandpaper. Clean pastels mean that you will have better results.

11. Container
To hold pencils and other supplies.

12. Small sponge
A damp sponge is essential to keep fingers clean while working so as to avoid smudging the painting.

13. Plastic container
For litter and pencil sharpenings.

Table easel

PAINTING PROCEDURE

These are the general guidelines for the method you will follow at the beginning of each painting project.

1. Sectioning the sandpaper or coloured paper
Use a pencil to draw the grids. If your paper is to be used vertically, draw three equally spaced vertical lines and five equally spaced horizontal lines. If your paper is to be used horizontally, draw five equally spaced vertical lines and three equally spaced horizontal lines. When doing this, a useful tip is to divide the paper into quarters first, then divide each section as indicated in the illustration. The sections do not have to be measured exactly. This method of sectioning-off the paper can be used for any size paper. On larger paper the squares will be larger but so will the scale of the drawing.

2. The drawing
For each project study the drawing carefully. Start at the bottom of the paper and mark a place for the objects before drawing them in. This helps with sizing and correct placement. Pencil in the drawing, which is a simplified form of the finished painting. The detail is put in later. Use the squares as guidelines. Put objects such as vases in a box, again using the squares as guidelines to make sure that both sides are equal. Decide where the light is coming from and pencil in the areas of shadow lightly. Erase any mistakes and then outline the objects and paint in the shadow areas lightly again but this time with the purple pastel pencil. *Don't outline the grid lines or they will show through the colour you add later.* Now erase the grid lines lightly and carefully. They were simply used to place your objects correctly. You will find that your pencil drawing will fade so you must outline it quickly with the purple pastel pencil. Make sure you don't outline the grids.

NOTE

One of the most difficult lessons to learn is when to stop. If you overwork your painting it will not only lose its spontaneity but you may very well lose the painting.

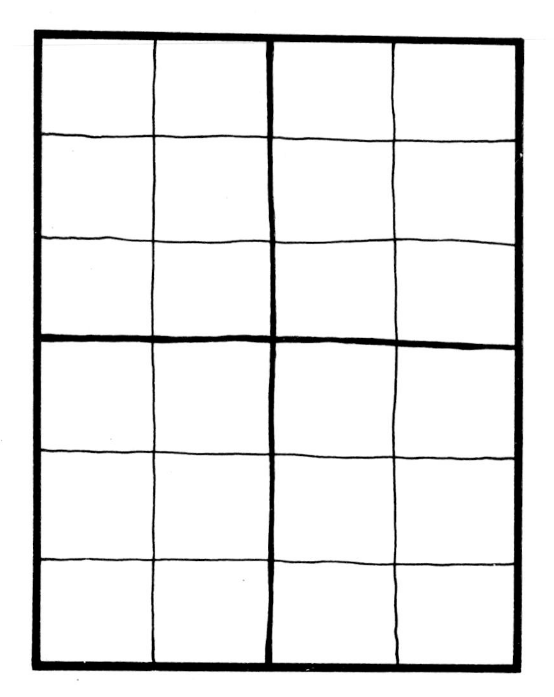

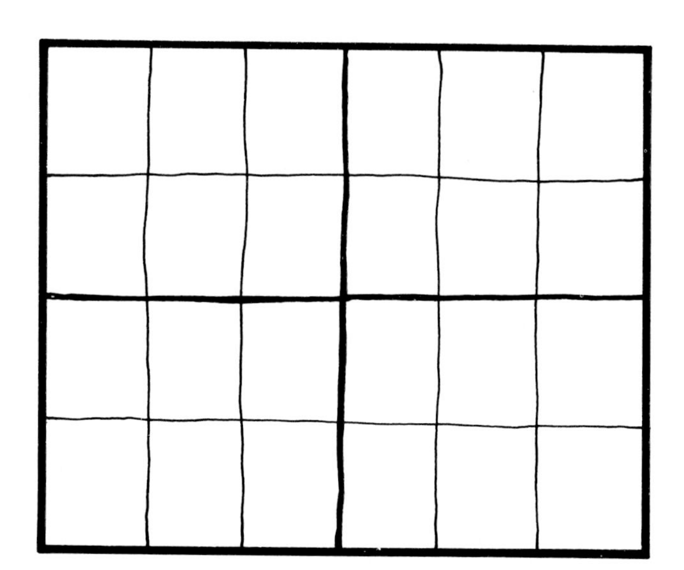

Mixed Bouquet

THE DRAWING

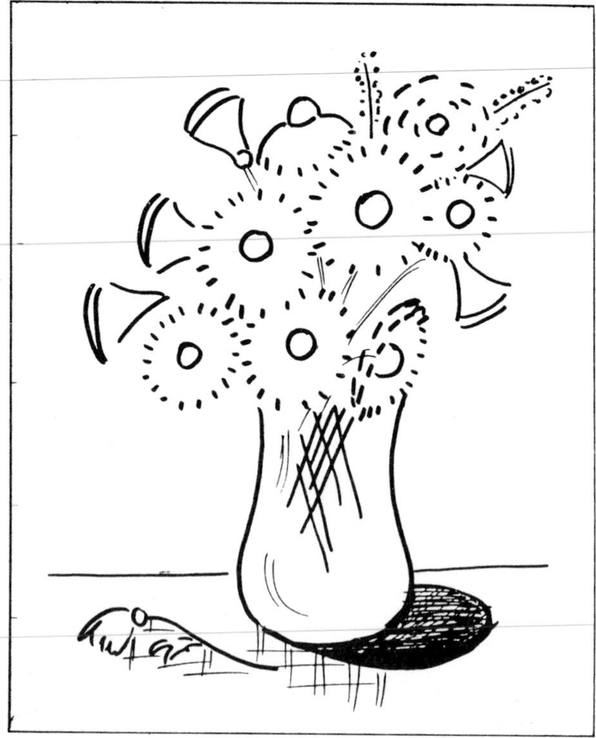

1. Use sandpaper 23×30cm (9×12in) placed vertically. (You can of course use a smaller or larger piece of sandpaper as long as you keep everything in proportion. By using the grid system your subject will be placed correctly.)

2. Study the painting and drawings on pages 13 and 14 carefully.

3. Draw the grid lines in pencil (see page 12) and then, also in pencil, sketch in the simplified picture as shown above left.

4. The light is coming from the left (note the shadows of the vase on the right) so lightly shade in the area on the right side of the vase with pencil.

5. Take the purple pastel pencil and outline the flowers and vase lightly as shown above right. Also lightly paint in the shadow with the purple pastel pencil. This preserves the essential part of the drawing. The rest of the pencil lines which you do not need will fade quickly as you work. (Do NOT draw the grid lines in purple.)

6. Erase all the grid lines, leaving the purple outline intact (see above right). Pencil lines are easily erased, but if they are outlined in purple pastel pencil they cannot be erased and will show through the background of the painting.

THE PAINTING

NOTE

As you work you will have to remove bits of the paper wrapper from the pastels. Make sure you match your pastels and their names with the squares of colour selected for each painting.

Background

Usually the background is put in first. However, in this painting the sandpaper itself provides the background.

Glass Vase

If the vase to be painted is opaque, such as pottery or china, then it is usually painted in before the flowers. Here, however, it will be painted in after the flowers as the stems are to be visible through the glass.

Flowers

1. Study the painting carefully. Because this is a multi-coloured floral, it makes sense and saves time to paint all the flowers of the same colour at one time. You can then go on to a second colour.

2. Study the three stages of the flower head illustrated before starting to paint, as this method can be applied to all the flowers whatever their colour. For vibrant colours press down hard on the pastels.

ORANGE FLOWERS

1. Study the orange flowers in the finished painting and in the step-by-step illustration.

2. You may find it easier to pencil in the petals lightly first, leaving the short purple strokes as shaded areas between the petals. Paint the dark tone (Red) in the area around the centre of the large orange flower.

3. Paint the right side of the flower in the medium tone (Orange).

4. Paint the left side in the light tone (Yellow Orange) and paint the tips of these petals with the extra light tone (Pale Orange).

5. Paint the left profile flower with the medium tone (Orange) around the centre. The tips are painted with the light tone (Yellow Orange) highlighted with the extra light tone (Pale Orange).

6. Paint the centre profile flower with the dark tone (Red) near the centre. Paint the right tips in the medium tone (Orange) and the left tips with the light tone (Yellow Orange) highlighted with the extra light tone (Pale Orange).

7. Paint the centres in Van Dyke Brown with a touch of Yellow as a highlight.

YELLOW FLOWERS

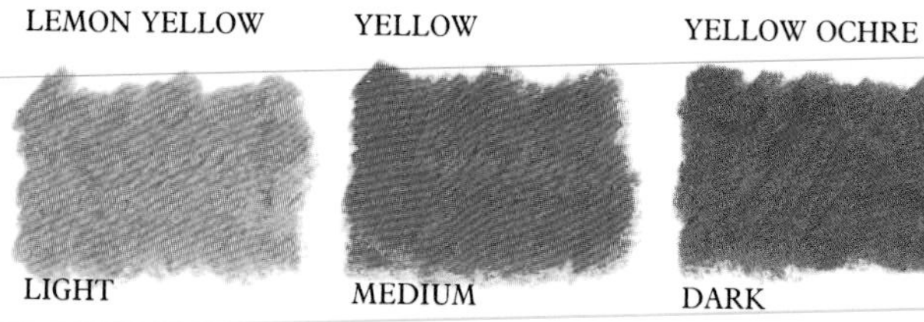

1. Study the yellow flowers in the finished painting.

2. Starting with the large flower, paint the dark tone (Yellow Ochre) in the area towards the centre.

3. Paint the right side of the flower in the medium tone (Yellow).

4. Paint the left side in the light tone (Lemon Yellow) and paint the tips of these with a little White.

5. Paint the centre in Van Dyke Brown with a highlight of Yellow.

6. The structure of the flower on the upper right is a little different. Look at it carefully. The strokes are round, but the same yellow tones are applied in the same areas, on the right and left sides, with the exception of the dark tone (Yellow Ochre) in the central area which is omitted. The centre is Van Dyke Brown.

7. The small yellow flower on the lower left has Red around the centre with touches of Orange on the right side and the medium tone (Yellow) on the left. The centre is Van Dyke Brown.

WHITE FLOWERS

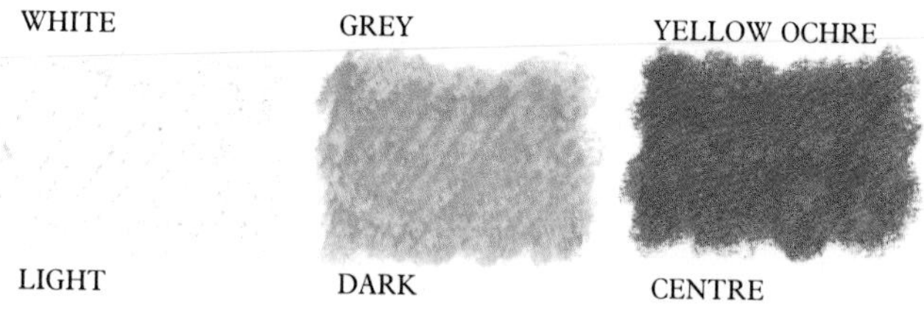

1. Study the white flowers in the finished painting.

2. The flower on the lower right is in semi-profile. Paint the area around the half centre in the dark tone (Grey).

3. Paint the short petals and the right side of the flower in the light tone (White).

4. Paint the centre in Yellow Ochre with a highlight of Yellow.

5. Paint the two profile flowers on either side by using the dark tone (Grey) near the stem and the light tone (White) on the tips.

BLUE FLOWERS

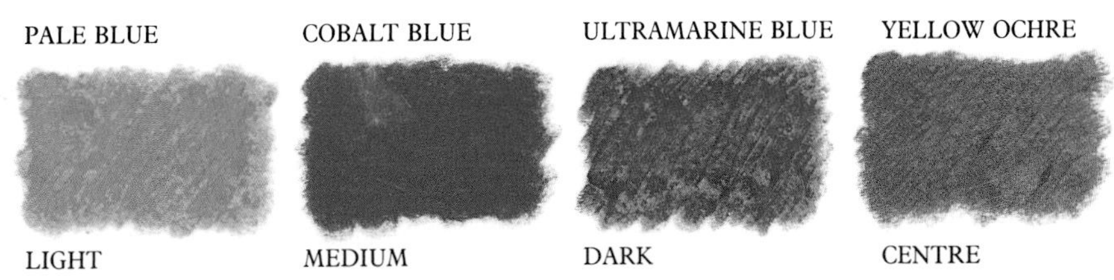

1. Study the blue flowers in the finished painting.

2. Paint the upper petals of the full blue flower in the dark tone (Ultramarine Blue).

3. Paint several petals on the right in the medium tone (Cobalt Blue) and the other petals in the light tone (Pale Blue). Paint the tips of the light tone with a little White.

4. Paint the centre in Yellow Ochre with a highlight of Yellow.

5. Paint the profile flowers with the light tone (Pale Blue) near the stem and the dark tone (Ultramarine Blue) on the outer petals.

6. Paint the small flowers on the spiked stems in the upper right corner as impressions rather than full flowers. Use the light and dark tones (Pale Blue and Ultramarine Blue).

LEAVES

1. Study the leaves in the finished painting and also the purple strokes you can see between the flowers.

2. Before painting in the leaves, carefully stroke Purple between the flowers and into the edges of the petals as shown. This creates depth and shadow.

3. The leaves are delicate and lacy; they look more like impressions than detailed illustrations. Paint the leaves on the right in the dark tone (Deep Green) and medium tone (Green). Keep the dark tone around the flowers and the medium on the outside edge.

4. Paint the leaves on the left (or light) side in the medium tone (Green) and the light tone (Yellow Green). Keep the medium tone around the flowers and the light tone on the edges. Tip this light tone with a highlight of Yellow.

STEMS

1. Study the finished painting. The stems in the vase should look as if they are crossed. Use the same tones as for the leaves.

2. Paint the tops of the stems in the dark tone (Deep Green) with the medium tone (Green) lower down and the light tone (Yellow Green) around the base.

3. Paint the green stem and a few leaves of the flower lying on the table. Paint the flower as an impression with some yellow and orange tones.

VASE

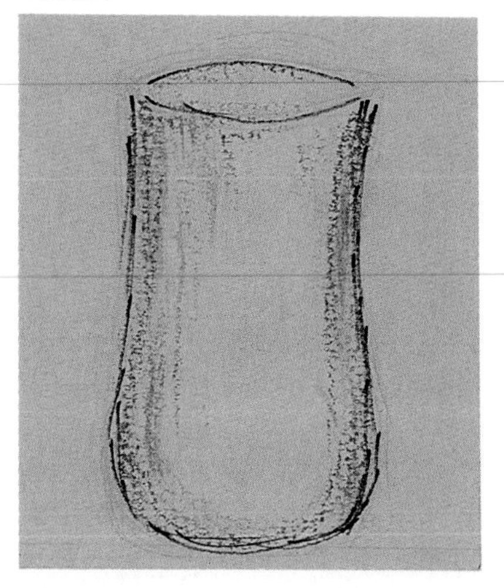

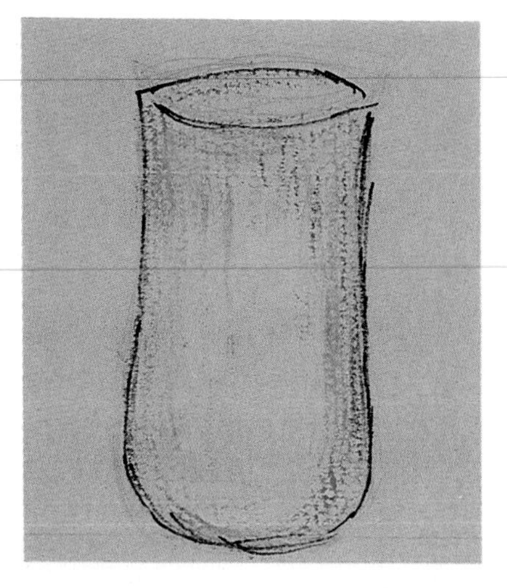

1. Study the vase in the finished painting and in the step-by-step illustration. Re-outline it in Purple.

2. Paint a very little Pale Blue around the inside edge of the vase and add White highlights where shown – on the sides and base of the vase and around the top, painting over the stems.

SHADOW

1. Study the finished painting.

2. Paint a soft line in Purple to give an impression of a table.

3. Paint the shadow of the vase on the right in Purple with highlights of blue and green tones.

Congratulations! You have finished your first project. It will get easier!

Summertime

THE DRAWING

1. Use sandpaper 23×30cm (9×12in) placed vertically.

2. Study the painting and drawings on pages 19 and 20 carefully.

3. Draw the grid lines in pencil (see page 12) and then, also in pencil, sketch in the simplified picture as shown above left.

4. The light is coming from the left (note the shadows of the objects on the right) so lightly shade in the areas on the ground and by the far tree in pencil.

5. Take the purple pastel pencil and outline the objects and paint in the shadow lightly as shown above right. This preserves the essential part of the drawing. The rest of the pencil lines which you do not need will fade quickly as you work. (Do NOT draw the grid lines in purple.)

6. Erase all the grid lines leaving the purple outline intact (see above right). Pencil lines are easily erased, but if they are outlined in purple pastel pencil they cannot be erased and will show through the background of the painting.

THE PAINTING

SKY

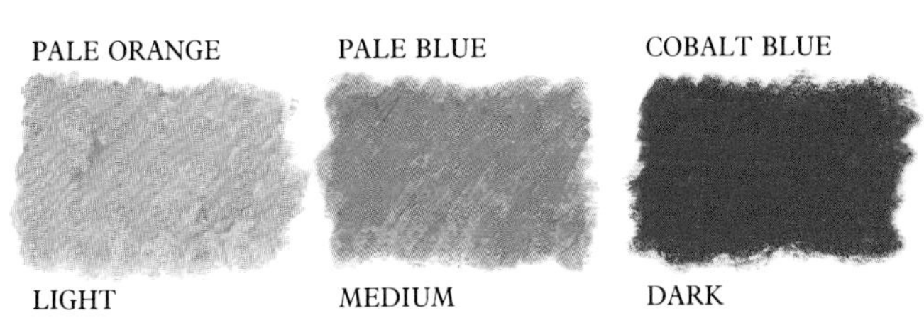

Note
Until you have a bit more experience it is easier to paint all your skies in a similar fashion. Use these instructions as general guidelines each time you want to paint a sky.

1. Study the finished painting.

2. Paint the light tone (Pale Orange) along the horizon in upward slanting strokes.

3. Add the medium tone (Pale Blue) to the rest of the sky using the same slanting strokes. The sandpaper should still show through.

4. Paint a very little dark tone (Cobalt Blue) at the top of the sky, blending it with the other tones.

5. Paint some white patches in the sky for clouds as shown.

MOUNTAINS

1. Study the finished painting. Notice that the mountains are formed by a soft undulating line and that there are no sharp points.

2. Lightly paint the dark tone (Purple) on the right side of the mountain. Use slanting downward strokes.

3. Paint the left (or light) side in the light tone (Light Purple) using slanting strokes again. Try to keep the colours soft and hazy, as the mountains are seen from a distance.

4. Add a little Pale Blue and Pink over the light tone (Light Purple) but be careful not to lose all the separate colours.

HILLS

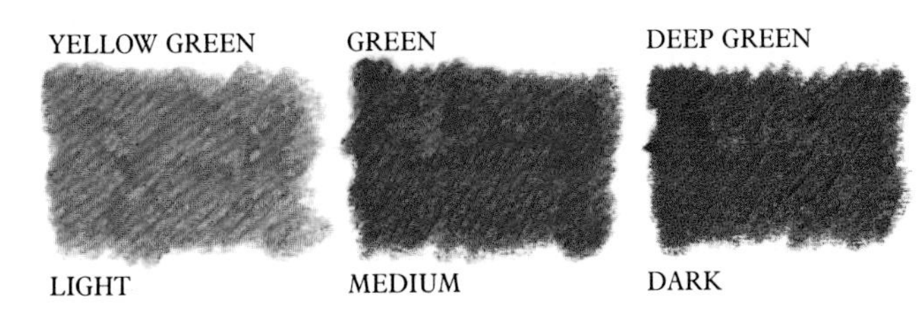

1. Study the finished painting.

2. Paint the right side of the hills in the medium tone (Green). Use the same slanting, downward strokes.

3. Paint the left (or light) side in the light tone (Yellow Green). Add Pale Blue and White lightly over the two tones to give the impression of distance.

4. Add some vegetation on the top of the hills using the dark tone (Deep Green) and soften it gently with Light Purple as shown. Stroke the same Purple at the base of the hills adding a little Deep Green as well.

FIELD

1. Study the finished painting. Use the same tones as for the hills.

2. Paint the field behind the fence in the light tone (Yellow Green). Use a horizontal stroke this time.

3. Paint Lemon Yellow over the Yellow Green on the left (or light) side.

4. To colour the field in front of the fence, paint alternate strokes of the dark and light tones (Deep Green and Yellow Green) as shown. Do not cover the area where the flowers are to go – if you do it will be difficult to achieve the bright tones required for the flowers.

5. Paint a little Purple and Deep Green in front of the flower area to create some shadow. Add some Purple shadows to the right side of the small trees in the distance also.

TREES

Note

These are general guidelines for painting trees. Read these carefully first before going on to the specific instructions for the trees in this picture.

1. Study the step-by-step illustration carefully.

2. Paint the structure of the tree in Van Dyke Brown. Outline it if necessary in black charcoal.

3. To paint the foliage add short strokes of the dark tone (here it is Deep Green) across the branches and trunk – see the first step.

4. Add similar strokes of medium tone (here, Green) on top of the dark tone – see the second step.

5. Use the light tone (here, Yellow Green) on the light side of the tree. In this illustration this is the left side. You can then add a lighter colour (e.g. White) as a highlight.

6. Paint a shadow under the dark side of the tree using Purple and the dark tone as shown. If you need extra shadow on the tree itself, add Purple underneath the tones.

LARGE TREE

1. Study the finished painting. Notice that there are 3 distinct 'layers' of leaves on this tree, separated by branches. Follow the basic instructions as above, keeping the areas apart. Use the colour tones illustrated above.

2. The light is falling on the left side of the tree. Therefore add the light tone (Yellow Green) to the left.

3. Use White as a highlight on the Yellow Green.

4. Add a little Purple beneath each layer to create some shadows.

5. Outline the trunk and branches again in black charcoal. It should be slightly darker on the right side. Use Brown and Blue to highlight the trunk and a little Pale Orange as highlight on the branches.

SMALL TREE

1. Study the finished picture. Notice that this is a group of three trees as seen from a distance, so outline the trunks very softly in black charcoal. Use the same tones as for the large trees.

2. Follow the basic instructions as above, blending the different tones together a little. Remember, however, to keep the dark tone (Deep Green) distinct on the right (shady) side and the light tone (Yellow Green) distinct on the left.

3. Add a very little Brown and Blue to the trunk and highlight with Pale Orange.

4. Highlight the foliage with Pale Orange as shown and add a few light strokes of black charcoal across the tree to give the impression of branches.

FENCE

BROWN VAN DYKE BROWN

LIGHT DARK

1. Study the finished painting.

2. Using the light tone (Brown), paint the top of the rails and the left side of the posts.

3. Paint the dark tone (Van Dyke Brown) on the front of the posts and underneath the light tone at the bottom of the rails. Add a very little Black over the Van Dyke Brown.

4. Paint highlights where indicated with Pale Orange and Blue.

FLOWERS

YELLOW

LIGHT

ORANGE

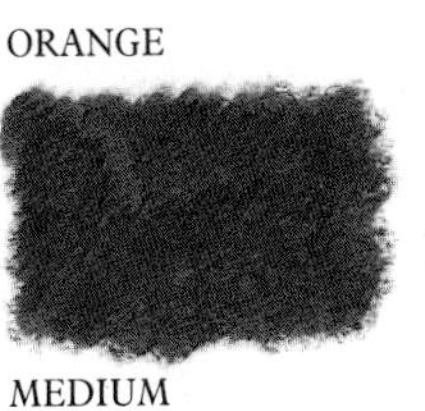

MEDIUM

RED

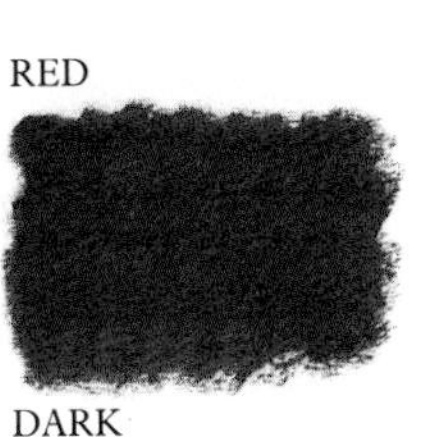

DARK

1. Study the finished painting.

2. Using the stated tones, paint impressions of flowers as shown. Press down hard on the pastels for vibrant colours. Add Yellow Green and Deep Green among the flowers to suggest leaves.

Vegetable Still Life

1. Use sandpaper 23×30cm (9×12in) placed horizontally.

2. Study the painting and drawings on pages 24 and 25 carefully.

3. Draw the grid lines in pencil (see page 12) and then, also in pencil, sketch in the simplified picture as shown opposite above.

4. The light is coming from the left (note the shadows of the objects on the right) so lightly shade those areas on the right in pencil.

5. Take the purple pastel pencil and outline the objects and paint in the shadow lightly as shown opposite below. (Do NOT draw the grid lines in purple pastel pencil.)

6. Erase all the grid lines, leaving the purple outline intact (see opposite below).

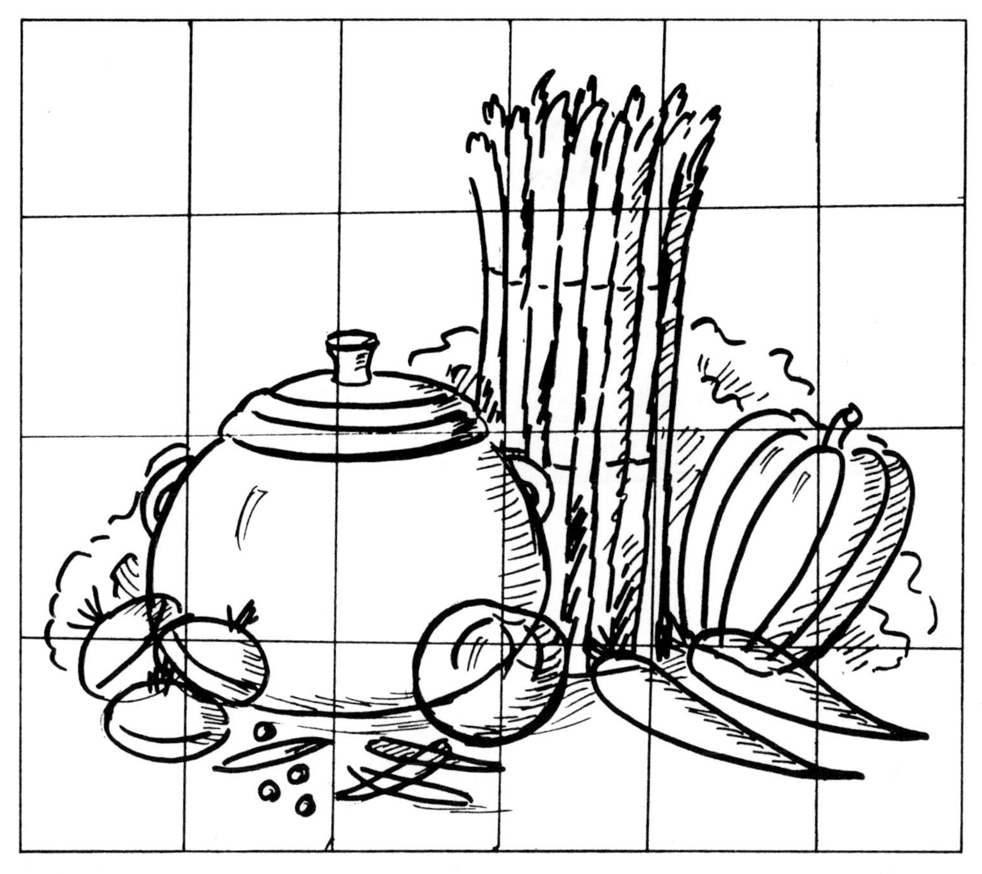

THE PAINTING

BACKGROUND

1. Study the finished painting. Note that the sandpaper forms most of the background and that there is very little colour to add.

2. Use the side of the Yellow Ochre pastel to paint the whole of the background in light vertical strokes. Paint up to and in front of the vegetables. Most of the sandpaper should still show through. You will, of course, have to remove the wrapper from the pastel to paint in this way.

PARSLEY

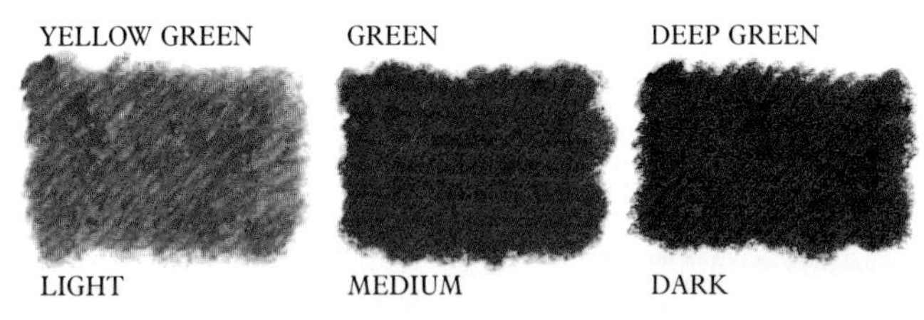

1. Study the finished painting. Note that objects in the background are always painted first.

2. Using short, round strokes paint the dark tone (Deep Green) around the pepper as far as the carrots. Paint the medium tone (Green) in the area above the pepper. Try to keep your strokes lacy and loose.

3. Using a little of the medium tone (Green) paint the parsley to the left of the asparagus and the soup tureen. Top it with the light tone (Yellow Green).

ASPARAGUS

1. Study the finished painting. Note that the asparagus stalks are not perfectly straight! Use the same tones as for the parsley.

2. Paint the stalks at the back in the dark tone (Deep Green). Note that they lean a little to the right. Try to keep your outlines soft.

3. Outline the right side of the stalks in front with the medium tone (Green). Fill in the stalks with Yellow Ochre. Note that the third stalk from the left has almost disappeared behind the others and has no tip. Paint this with the dark tone (Deep Green) and a little Yellow Ochre. Try to make the stalks slightly uneven. Shade a little Purple between the front stalks.

4. Using Deep Green and Yellow Ochre paint two braided strings around the asparagus. Add a rounded Purple shadow where the tureen stands in front of the asparagus.

SOUP TUREEN

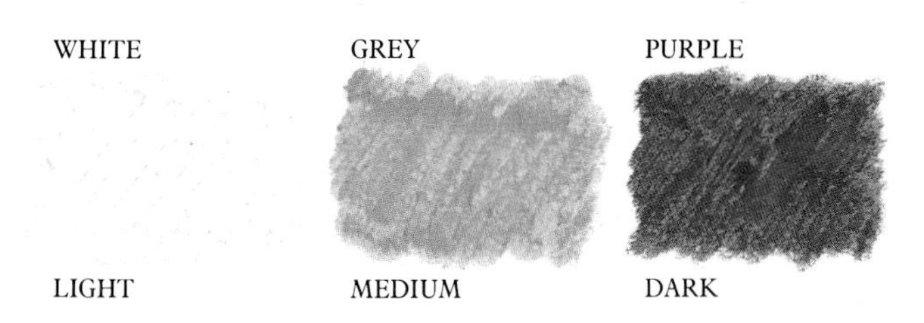

1. Study the finished painting and the step-by-step illustration. Keep your strokes rounded, following the lines of the tureen. This way you will achieve the form and texture of porcelain.

2. With horizontal strokes, paint the tureen in the medium tone (Grey).

3. Outline the tureen again with the purple pastel pencil. Shade the right side and bottom of the tureen in Purple. Take care with the lid and lid handle.

4. Using curved strokes, add highlights in White to the left side of the tureen as shown. They should be painted about 2cm (1in) into the tureen, on the lid, lid handle and on the tops of the two side handles. Take care as these highlights are important.

PEPPER

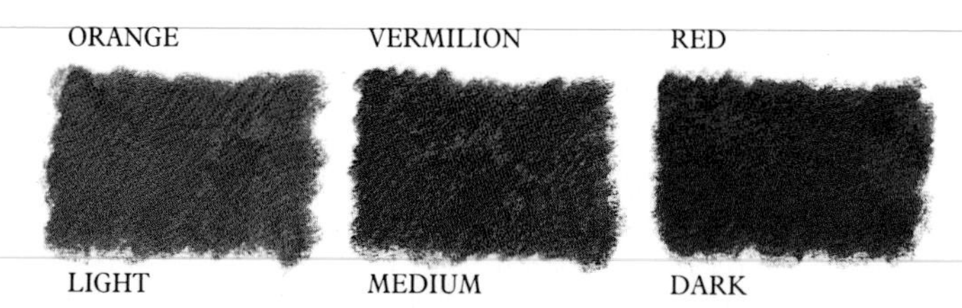

1. Study the finished painting and the step-by-step illustration. Notice that the pepper is painted in 'sections'.

2. Paint the bottom, left and right sides of the pepper in the dark tone (Red), as shown in the first step. Outline each section in the same tone. Paint the area around the stem with the dark tone (Red) on the left and the medium tone (Vermilion) on the right.

3. Use the medium tone (Vermilion) to paint the 3 middle sections as shown in the second step. Paint a little Vermilion in the left section and a little more in the centre section. The right section is mostly Vermilion.

4. Using the light tone (Orange), paint in the remainder. Be careful not to lose the other tones.

5. Paint the curved stem in Black pastel with a touch of Green.

6. Paint the White highlights on the pepper as shown.

TOMATO

1. Study the finished painting. Use the same colours as for the pepper.

2. Paint the right side and bottom of the tomato in the dark tone (Red).

3. Paint the centre in the medium tone (Vermilion).

4. Paint the light tone (Orange) on the left (or light) side.

5. Paint the stem with Deep Green on the right side and Yellow Green on the left side, giving the impression of sections.

6. Add White highlights where shown.

CARROTS

1. Study the finished painting.

2. Using slightly curved strokes, paint the right side and top of the carrots in the dark tone (Vermilion).

3. Paint the medium tone (Orange) and the light tone (Yellow) on the extreme left. Make the carrots look uneven.

4. Add a wavy line of Lemon Yellow down the centre of the carrots as a highlight.

5. Paint the leafy tops of the carrots with Deep Green and Yellow Green as shown.

6. Add a touch of Pale Blue at the top of the carrots and a little Purple as shadow.

ONIONS

1. Study the finished painting.

2. Paint the onions in the medium tone (Yellow Ochre).

3. Add dark tone (Brown) to the right side and the bottom of the onions.

4. Paint the highlight in the light tone (Pale Orange) with small curved strokes across the centre of the onion.

5. Paint the onion tops in the dark and light tones.

SHADOWS

1. Study the shadows in the finished picture. Paint Purple shadows under and around the vegetables and soup tureen as shown. Be careful to leave some space to paint the peapods.

PEAS

1. Study the finished painting. Use the same tones as for the parsley.

2. Paint the right side of the peapods in the medium tone (Green) and outline with a little Purple.

3. Paint the left side in the light tone (Yellow Green) and add a few highlights of White as shown.

4. The single peas on the table are painted with the medium tone (Green) on the right and the light tone (Yellow Green) on the left. Add tiny touches of White as highlights and some Purple underneath as shadow.

First Snow

1. Use sandpaper 23×30cm (9×12in) placed horizontally.

2. Study the painting and drawings on pages 30 and 31 carefully.

3. Draw the grid lines in pencil (see page 12) and then, also in pencil, sketch in the simplified picture as shown opposite above. You can also refer to the first step of the step-by-step illustration on page 33 for hints on sketching in the house.

4. The light is coming from the left (note the shadows of the objects on the right) so lightly shade in these areas with pencil.

5. Take the purple pastel pencil and outline the objects and paint in the shadow lightly as shown opposite below. Don't outline the top branches of the large trees – you will paint in the sky first and then add the branches. Also, don't outline the fence – you will paint this in at the end.

6. Erase all the grid lines, the fence and the top branches of the large trees, leaving the purple outline intact (see opposite below).

THE PAINTING

SKY

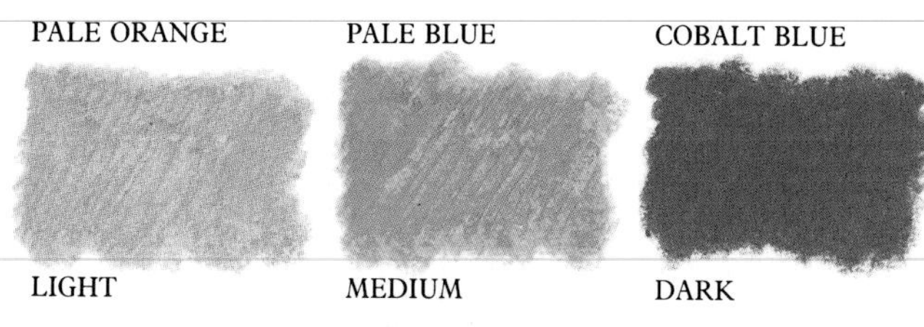

1. Study the finished painting.

2. Using upward strokes, paint the light tone (Pale Orange) along the long bank of trees on the horizon.

3. Paint the rest of the sky in the medium tone (Pale Blue). Use the same upward strokes.

4. Paint a little dark tone (Cobalt Blue) at the top of the sky and blend it with the other tones.

5. With the purple pastel pencil draw in the tops of the trees which you earlier erased.

BANK OF TREES ON HORIZON

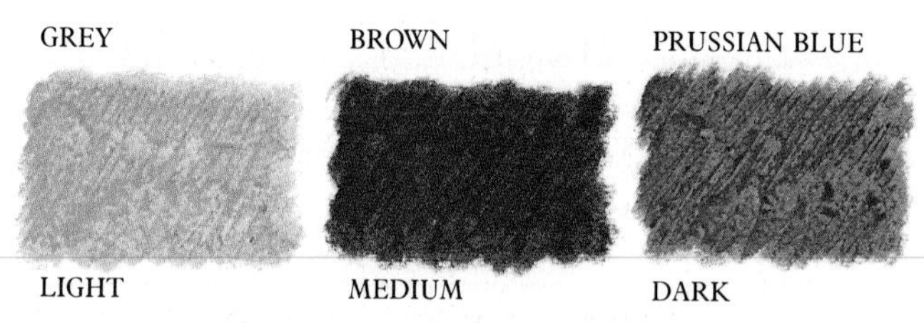

1. Study the finished painting. Note that the trees are uneven in height and are hazy and indistinct. They should be painted as impressions rather than definite outlines.

2. Using upward strokes of uneven height, paint the dark tone (Prussian Blue) at the base of the bank of trees. Be careful not to make your strokes too long.

3. Layer the medium tone (Brown) over the top half of the Prussian Blue lines.

4. With the light tone (Grey) paint the tops of the trees. Again, try to keep the trees at varying heights. Add a little Purple to the Grey.

HOUSE

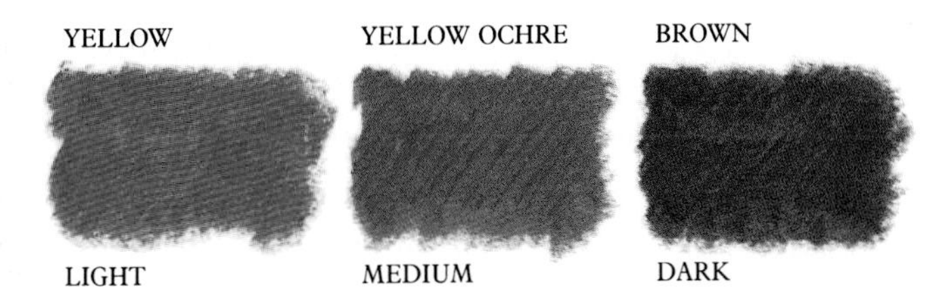

1. Study the finished painting and the step-by-step illustration. Note that the roof will be painted in at a later stage.

2. Paint the front of the house in the medium tone (Yellow Ochre) with a touch of the dark tone (Brown) under the eaves. Add Purple to the eaves as shown in the first step. Paint the front of the wood shed in the same tones.

3. Paint the side of the house and the wood shed in the light tone (Yellow), shading a little dark tone (Brown) at the bottom. Paint the chimneys in the dark and light tones (Brown and Yellow).

4. Paint the windows with black charcoal pencil and touches of Pale Blue and Orange. Keep the outlines soft and hazy.

5. Add Pale Blue and White to the house as highlights where shown.

SNOW

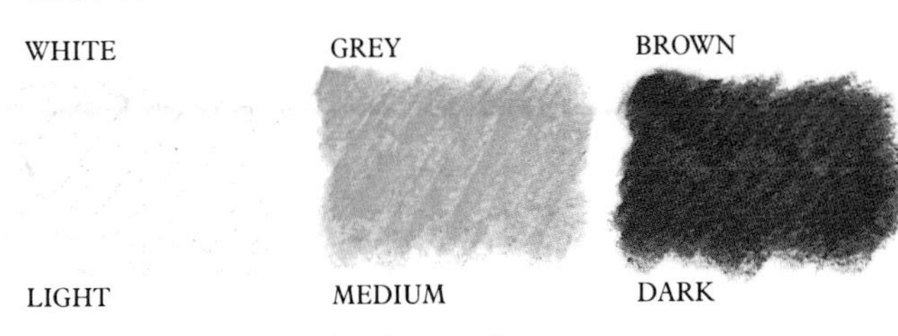

1. Study the finished painting.

2. Use a very little of the dark tone (Brown) to paint the ruts in the road. Soften them with the medium tone (Grey), especially around the deep rut on the right. This gives the impression of the house being set slightly above the road. Highlight with a very little Pale Blue. Darken the ruts here and there with the black charcoal pencil.

3. Paint the medium tone (Grey) across the bottom of the painting and over the left side around the large trees.

4. Paint the light tone (White) over the mound on the right side, and the road and ground on the left. Use horizontal strokes and press down hard on the pastel for a strong colour. Blend the White in with the Grey where the two colours meet.

ROOF

1. Study the finished painting. Use the same tones as for the snow.

2. Paint the light tone (White) over the roof of the house and wood shed. Add a touch of medium tone (Grey) to the left side of the roof to form the shadow.

TREES AROUND THE HOUSE

1. Study the finished picture.

2. Outline the trees with the black charcoal pencil. Using short, fan-like strokes paint the tops of the branches in Brown. Add strokes of White and a little Pale Blue as highlight.

LARGE FOREGROUND TREES

1. Study the finished picture.

2. Paint the left side of the trees in the dark tone (Brown) and the right side in the light tone (Grey). Outline the trees with the black charcoal pencil. The trees should look graceful.

3. Highlight the branches with Pale Orange and Pale Blue as shown.

FENCE

1. Study the finished painting. Note that the fence is broken and uneven.

2. Using delicate, uneven strokes paint the fence with the black charcoal pencil.

3. Add a little Pale Blue as a highlight.

4. Using White, paint a faint impression of smoke coming out of the chimney.

Pink Shrub Rose

THE DRAWING

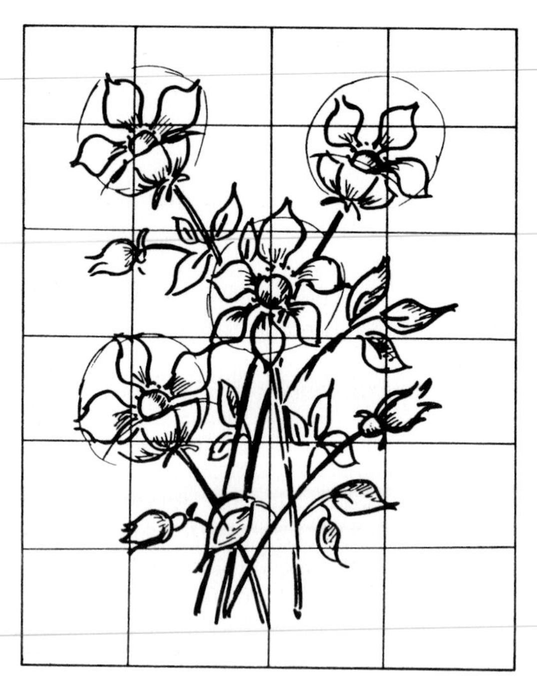

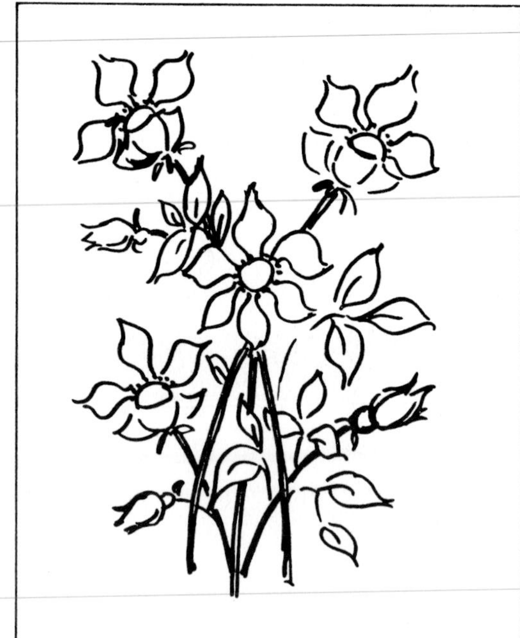

1. Use sandpaper 23×30cm (9×12in) placed vertically.

2. Study the painting and drawings on pages 35 and 36 carefully.

3. Draw the grid lines in pencil, and then, also in pencil, sketch in the simplified picture as shown above left. You can pencil in some circles to help you place the flower heads.

4. The light is coming from the left (note the shadows on the right of the flowers and leaves) so lightly pencil in these areas.

5. Take the purple pastel pencil and outline the objects lightly as shown above right. (Do NOT draw the grid lines in purple.)

6. Erase all the grid lines, leaving the purple outline intact (see above right).

THE PAINTING

BACKGROUND

1. Study the finished painting. Note that the background colour is very light.

2. Using Light Purple, lightly shade in the area between the flowers. Use the side, not the tip, of the pastel.

FLOWERS

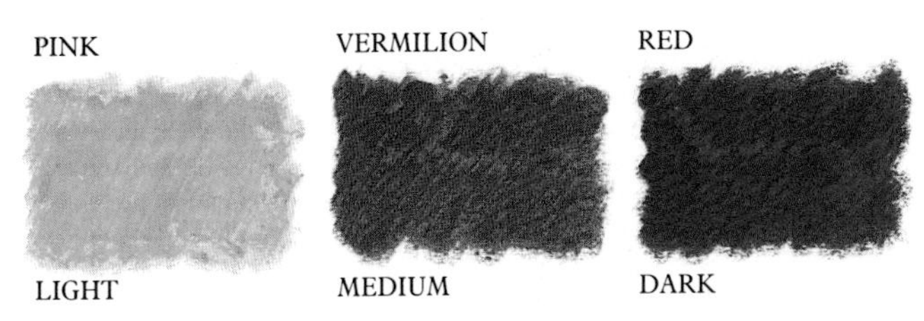

1. Study the finished painting. Start by painting the inside edges of the petals first.

2. Using short strokes, paint the area around the stamens in the medium tone (Vermilion).

3. Paint the rest of the petals in the light tone (Pink). Note that the lower petals on the two uppermost flowers are in 3 'sections'. Paint the right side of each section in the dark tone (Red). Add the medium tone (Vermilion) to the middle and a touch of Pink to the left.

4. Outline all the flowers in the dark tone (Red). Try to keep your strokes fluid – the petals should not look static. Paint the little buds in the light tone (Pink), outlined in the medium tone (Vermilion).

CENTRES, LEAVES AND STEMS

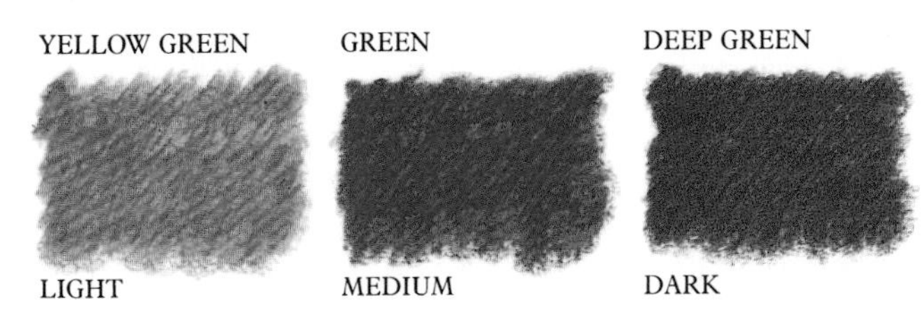

1. Study the finished painting.

2. Using round strokes, paint the centres using the light tone (Yellow Green) on the right and Lemon Yellow on the left. Paint the stamens as purple dots around the centres.

3. The top parts of the stems are painted in the dark tone (Deep Green) with the light tone (Yellow Green) over it. The bottoms of the stems are painted in the medium tone (Green). Add a little Purple at the very top of the stems as they are shaded by the flowers.

4. Paint the leaves underneath the flower heads in the dark and light tones (Deep Green and Yellow Green).

5. Paint the leaves on the right (or dark) side partly in the dark tone (Deep Green) and partly in the medium tone (Green). Try to make the leaves look delicate.

6. Paint the leaves on the left (or light) side partly in the medium tone (Green) and partly in the light tone (Yellow Green). Paint the green buds in the dark tone (Deep Green) with Yellow Green in the centre.

As you have seen, this wasn't quite as complicated as some of the earlier ones!

Rocky Cove

1. Use sandpaper 23×30cm (9×12in) placed horizontally.

2. Study the painting and drawings on pages 38 and 39 carefully.

3. Draw the grid lines in pencil and then, also in pencil, sketch in the simplified picture as shown opposite above.

4. The light is coming from the left (note the shadows on the right of the objects) so lightly shade these areas in pencil.

5. Take the purple pastel pencil and outline the objects and paint in the shadow lightly as shown opposite below. (Do NOT draw the grid lines in purple.)

6. Erase all the grid lines, leaving the purple outline intact (see opposite below).

THE DRAWING

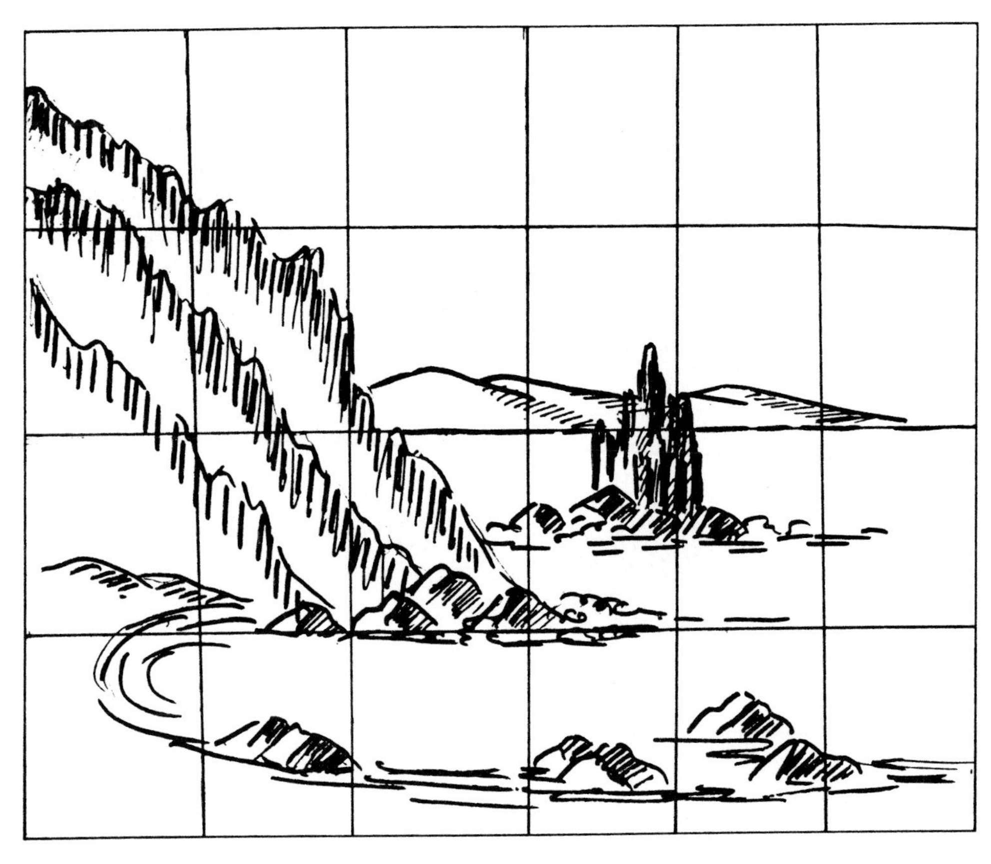

THE PAINTING

SKY

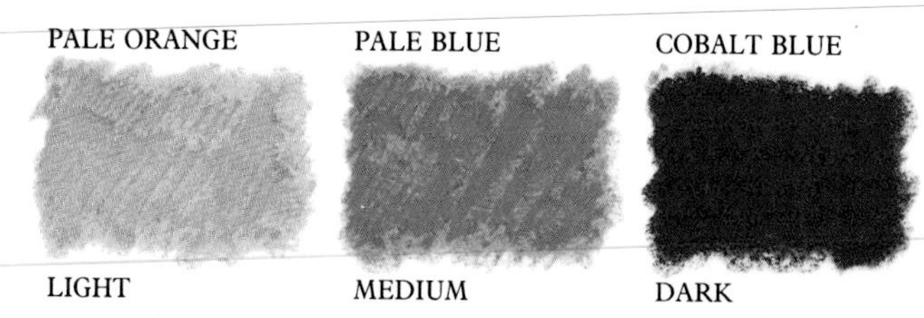

1. Study the finished painting. Note that, as it is sundown, there are warm tones on the rocks and cliffs.

2. Using upward, slanting strokes paint the light tone (Pale Orange) along the top of the mountains.

3. Add the medium tone (Pale Blue) to the rest of the sky – use the same slanting, upward strokes. Paint a little of the dark tone (Cobalt Blue) along the top of the sky and blend it with the Pale Blue.

4. Using White, paint an impression of clouds drifting across the sky. Stroke the pastel from right to left.

MOUNTAINS

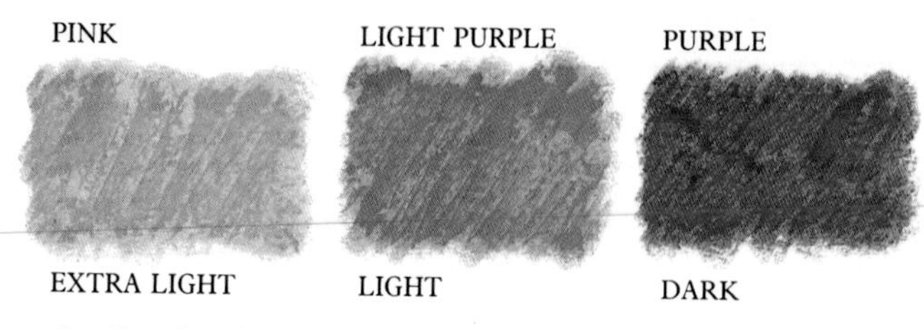

1. Study the finished painting.

2. Paint the dark tone (Purple) on the right (or dark) side of the mountains.

3. Paint the light tone (Light Purple) on the left side. Add a touch of Pink over the Light Purple. Highlight with a little Pale Blue.

CLIFF

1. Study the finished painting. Note that the cliff is painted in 3 rough 'sections' – see second drawing.

2. Using strong, vertical strokes, paint the top section in the dark tone (Green Grey). Add Purple over this. Use the medium tone (Green) to paint the vegetation at the top and highlight with the light tone (Yellow Green).

3. Paint the middle section the same way, but add the extra light tone (Pale Orange) as a separate section at the top. Use a little Orange to highlight.

4. Paint the last section in the same way as the first, using the dark tone (Green Grey) with Purple painted over it. Keep the strokes jagged. Again add the extra light tone to the far left and highlight it with Orange. Use the light tone (Yellow Green) to paint the vegetation.

5. Use short strokes of Pale Blue and Purple as a final highlight over the cliff as shown.

BEACH

1. Study the finished painting. Use the same tones as for the cliff.

2. Paint the beach, including the area between the rocks, with the extra light tone (Pale Orange). The sandpaper should still show through. Add a little Orange also.

3. Paint Purple shadows on the right side of the rocks.

4. Using the light tone (Yellow Green) and Purple, paint some vegetation along the left side of the beach.

ROCKS

1. Study the finished painting and the step-by-step illustration. Paint the large rock formation in the sea first.

2. Using vertical strokes, paint most of the rock in the dark tone (Van Dyke Brown). See the first step for details.

3. Paint the medium tone (Prussian Blue) over it, keeping it mostly to the right side. See the second stage and finished picture.

4. Paint the rocks at the base of the formation in the dark and medium tones (Van Dyke Brown and Prussian Blue).

5. Fill in the left side of the formation with the light tone (Pale Orange). Add a few jagged vertical strokes of Orange as a highlight.

6. Highlight the right side of the formation with a little black charcoal pencil and Pale Blue.

7. Paint the three rocks at the base of the cliff in the dark and medium tones (Van Dyke Brown and Prussian Blue). Add some Purple beneath them as shadow and a touch of Pale Blue as highlight.

8. Paint the rocks on the beach with the dark and medium tones (Van Dyke Brown and Prussian Blue) on the right side and the light tone (Pale Orange) on the left. Highlight the left side with a little Orange. Add Pale Blue as a further overall highlight.

SEA

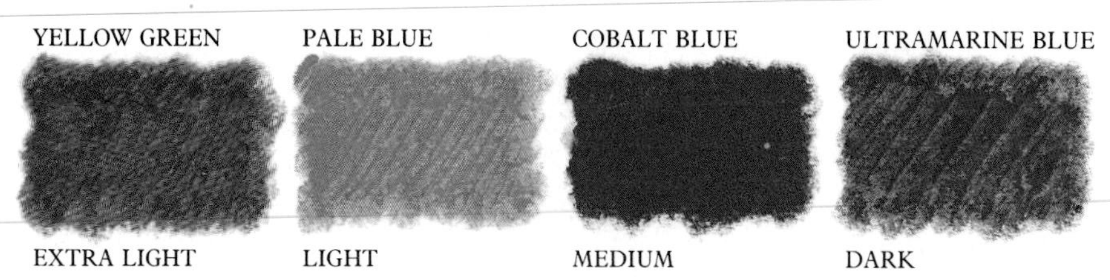

1. Study the finished painting. Paint the sea in 3 horizontal 'sections' – behind the rock formation, up to the rocks at the side of the cliff and up to the beach.

2. Paint the sea along the horizon in the dark tone (Ultramarine Blue). Shade the medium and light tones (Cobalt Blue and Pale Blue) in strips up to the rock formation.

3. In the middle section paint the dark tone (Ultramarine Blue) on the right side shading to the medium and light tones (Cobalt Blue and Pale Blue) towards the base of the cliff.

4. In the last section paint the dark tone (Ultramarine Blue) on the right. Paint the extra light tone (Yellow Green) on the left and on to the beach, and shade the medium and light tones (Cobalt Blue and Pale Blue) between them. You need a lighter colour at the shoreline because the water is shallow. Use light, alternate strokes, mixing up the tones. Take care, however, not to lose the tonal values completely.

SEA FOAM

1. With a clean White pastel paint the white foam as shown. Drag the tip of the White pastel through the front and middle sections of the sea.

The Blue Hat

THE DRAWING

1. Use sandpaper 23×30cm (9×12in) placed vertically.

2. Study the painting and drawings on pages 43 and 44 carefully.

3. Draw the grid lines in pencil, and then, also in pencil, sketch in the simplified picture as shown above left.

4. The light is coming from the right (note the shadows on the left of the objects) so lightly shade in these areas in pencil. (The shadow on the path is coming from another wall out of the picture.)

5. Take the purple pastel pencil and outline the objects and paint in the shadow lightly as shown above right. (Do NOT draw the grid lines in purple.)

6. Erase all the grid lines, leaving the purple outline intact (see above right).

THE PAINTING

SKY

1. Study the finished picture.

2. Paint the sky in Pale Blue. The sandpaper should still show through. Paint a little White in upward slanting strokes just above the wall.

WALL

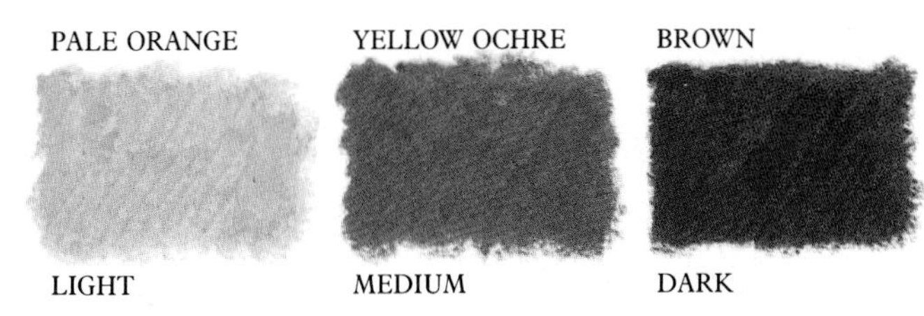

1. Study the finished picture.

2. Using horizontal strokes paint the entire wall in the medium tone (Yellow Ochre). The sandpaper should still show through.

3. Paint the left (or dark) side of the wall with the dark tone (Brown) but be careful not to lose the Yellow Ochre completely. Paint Brown along the top of the wall also. Note that this line should be uneven. Paint a few touches of Green on top of the wall as shown.

4. Stroke a little of the light tone (Pale Orange) on the right side of the wall and onto the wall above the bench.

PATH

1. Study the finished painting. Use the same tones as for the wall.

2. Using horizontal strokes paint the right (or dark) side of the path in the medium tone (Yellow Ochre). Shade it with Purple and Green Grey as shown. The edge of the shadow should not be straight.

3. Using horizontal strokes again, paint the left side of the path in the light tone (Pale Orange). Add a little of the medium tone (Yellow Ochre) to the left and bottom of the path.

BENCH

1. Study the finished painting.

2. Paint the top and legs of the bench in the light tone (Pale Orange). Paint the shadows of the hat and book in Purple where shown.

3. Add some Purple to the top of the legs – they are shaded by the overhang of the bench.

4. Paint a shadow under the bench with the dark tone (Brown). Add some Purple to this and also paint a little Purple under the left side of the bench and to the left side of it.

THE ARBOR

1. Study the finished painting.

2. Paint the arbor in Pale Orange. Be careful with the perspective.

3. Paint a little of the arbor showing through the leaves at the top as shown.

VINE

1. Study the finished painting. Note that the leaves are only impressions and not detailed. Your strokes should be lacy and loose. Study the 2 drawings and the finished painting carefully. Notice how the vine is broken down into 'sections'.

2. Paint the far left of the vine, including the part on the wall, in the dark tone (Deep Green) with a few touches of the medium tone (Green) and the light tone (Yellow Green).

3. Paint the left side of the left curve in the dark tone (Deep Green). Shade this to the medium tone (Green) in the middle and the light tone (Yellow Green) on the right. Paint the top of the vine in Deep Green and Green, highlighted with Yellow Green.

4. Paint the right of the vine with the light tone (Yellow Green). Add a little dark tone (Deep Green) to the tips of the leaves. Separate the sections a little with Purple.

5. To paint the small bush on the right, stroke the dark tone (Deep Green) on the left side. Add the medium tone (Green) to the middle and the light tone (Yellow Green) to the right.

6. Stroke a little Brown in between the sections of vine and also underneath it.

7. Paint Light Purple on to the wall as shown, which is the shadow made by the vine.

8. Paint the branches of the vine in Brown. They are mostly on the left. Keep your strokes long and graceful. Accent the branches here and there with the black charcoal pencil. Add White as a highlight where shown.

PLANT BEDS

1. Study the finished painting. Note that the beds are not flat and that the plants are impressions and not detailed. Use the same tones as for the vine.

2. Using short strokes, paint the beds on the left with the dark tone (Deep Green). Add the medium tone (Green) on top and paint a little light tone (Yellow Green) on the edges.

3. Paint the left side of the bed on the right with the dark tone (Deep Green). Add the medium tone (Green) to the middle and the light tone (Yellow Green) to the right. Blend the colours but don't lose the tonal values completely. Add a few strokes of Purple to accent the dark tone as shown.

HAT

1. Study the finished picture.

2. Paint the left side and bottom of the hat in the dark tone (Cobalt Blue).

3. Paint the rest of the hat in the light tone (Pale Blue).

BOOK

1. Study the finished picture.

2. Paint the cover of the book in Brown and the edges in Orange.

3. Paint a little White on the sides of the book for pages. Outline lightly in black charcoal pencil, if necessary.

Springtime in New York

1. Use light blue Ingres pastel paper or sugar (construction) paper 23×30cm (9×12in) placed horizontally.

2. Study the painting and drawings on pages 47 and 48 carefully.

3. Draw the grid lines in pencil and then, also in pencil, sketch in the simplified picture as shown overleaf above.

4. The light is coming from the right (note the shadows on the left of the trees) so lightly shade in these areas in pencil.

5. Take the purple pastel pencil and outline the objects and paint in the shadow lightly as shown overleaf below. (Do NOT draw the grid lines in purple.)

6. Erase all the grid lines, leaving the purple outline intact (see overleaf below).

THE DRAWING

THE PAINTING

BACKGROUND LAWN

1. Study the finished painting.

2. Paint the right side of the lawn behind the trees in the medium tone (Green Grey). Use horizontal strokes. Stroke a little Purple over the Green Grey, but don't cover it completely.

3. Paint the left side of the background lawn in the light tone (Yellow Green) and paint the extra light tone (Lemon Yellow) over it.

4. Paint a faint impression of more trees in the background by stroking the dark tone (Deep Green) just below the branches of the white tree. With light, short strokes paint Green Grey, Deep Green and Purple above the white tree and a very little Green Grey and Yellow Green above the pink tree. Patches of the blue paper should still show through.

PATH BEHIND TREES

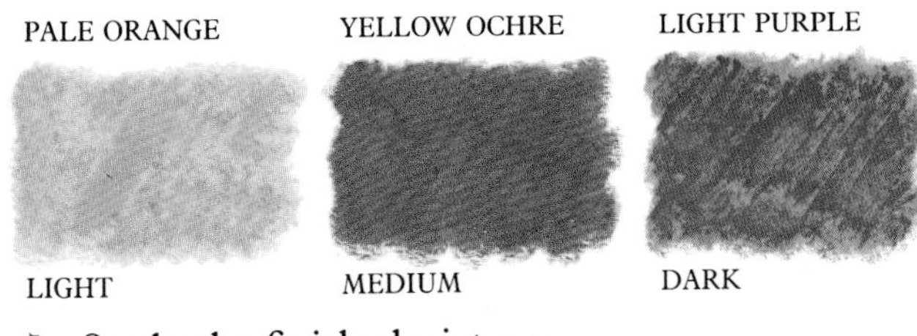

1. Study the finished picture.

2. Paint the far right of the horizontal path in the medium tone (Yellow Ochre), as far as the white tree.

3. Paint the middle section of the path in the light tone (Pale Orange).

4. Paint the far left of the path with the medium tone (Yellow Ochre). Paint the dark tone (Light Purple) over it.

FOREGROUND LAWN

1. Study the finished picture. Note that the lawn is split into left and right 'sections' by the narrow path running between the trees. Use the same tones as for the background lawn.

2. Paint the right side of the lawn around the white tree with the dark tone (Deep Green). Shade the far right in the medium tone (Green Grey). Add Purple to the Deep Green under the tree, but be careful not to lose the tonal values.

3. Paint the small bush on the right in the dark tone (Deep Green). Tip it with the medium tone (Green Grey).

4. Paint the left side of the lawn around the pink tree with the dark tone (Deep Green). Shade this to the light tone (Yellow Green) at the front of the lawn. Add Purple to the Deep Green under the tree but be careful not to lose the tonal values.

PATH BETWEEN TREES

1. Study the finished picture. Note that the path is wider at the far right than in the centre, where it meets the larger path.

2. Very lightly paint an impression of stones with a little Green. Paint a little Grey on the stones at the top of the path, and Lemon Yellow on the bottom stones. Keep your strokes soft so that the path is rather indistinct.

WHITE TREE

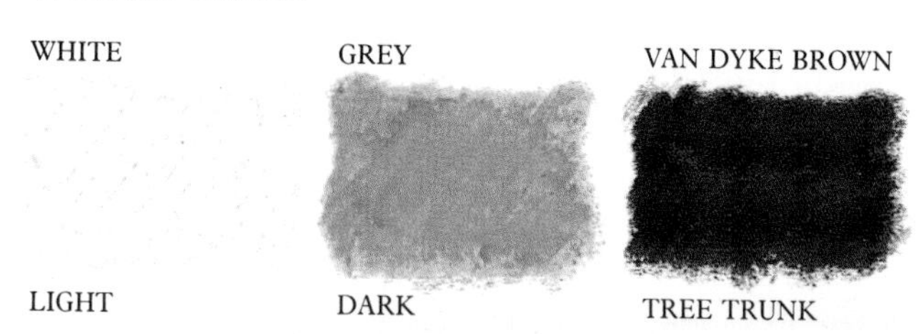

1. Study the finished picture and the step-by-step illustration for the pink tree. The same method applies to both trees. The blossom is painted in 'layers' as were the leaves of the trees you have painted previously. Note that the white tree, being further away, is slightly smaller than the pink tree.

2. Paint the trunk and lower branches in Van Dyke Brown. Outline the trunk here and there with the black charcoal pencil for accent.

3. Paint the bottom of each layer of blossom in the dark tone (Grey). Keep your strokes fan-like and slightly separate.

4. Paint the tops of the layers in White. Use the same fan-like strokes to make the blossom look soft.

5. Use the Van Dyke Brown to paint a few delicate branches through the blossom as shown. Accent the branches here and there with black charcoal pencil.

PINK TREE

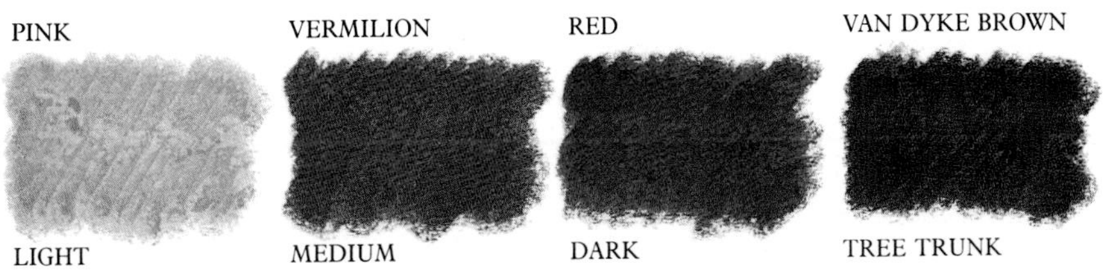

1. Study the finished painting and the step-by-step illustration. Note that the 'layers' of blossom can also be divided into left and right sides – the left being the dark (or shady) side. Make sure that you allow some blue paper to show through the blossom for sky. Paint the trunk and lower branches in Van Dyke Brown. Outline the trunk and branches here and there with the black charcoal pencil. Try to give the tree a 'gnarled' look. Highlight the base of the tree and the branches on the right with Pale Orange and the left side with Pale Blue.

2. Paint the layers of blossom on the left side with the dark tone (Red) at the bottom and the medium tone (Vermilion) at the top.

3. Paint the layers of blossom on the right with the medium tone (Vermilion) on the bottom and the light tone (Pink) at the top. Highlight these blossoms with White.

4. Use the Van Dyke Brown to paint a few delicate branches here and there with black charcoal pencil.

This is an especially lovely painting and well worth the effort.

Sailing on Lake Como

1. Use light blue Ingres paper or sugar (construction) paper 23×30cm (9×12in) placed horizontally.

2. Study the painting and drawings on pages 52 and 53 carefully.

3. Draw the grid lines in pencil and then, also in pencil, sketch in the simplified picture as shown opposite above.

4. The light is coming from the right (note the shadows on the left of the mountains) so lightly shade in these areas in pencil.

5. Take the purple pastel pencil and outline the objects and paint in the shadow lightly as shown opposite below. (Do NOT draw the grid lines in purple.)

6. Erase all the grid lines, leaving the purple outline intact (see opposite below).

THE PAINTING

SKY

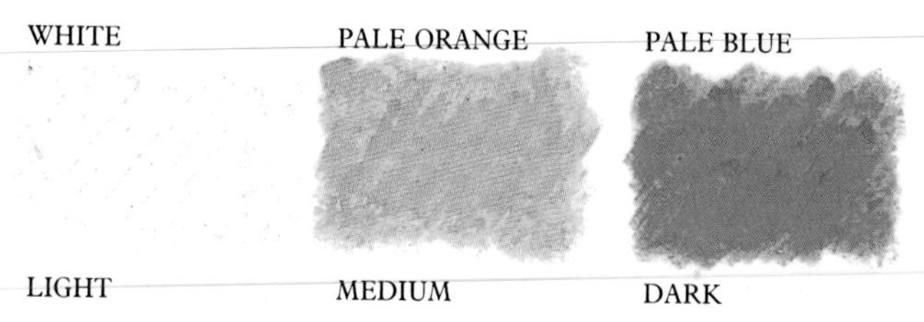

1. Study the finished painting.

2. Paint Pale Orange along the mountains with upward slanting strokes.

3. Paint the rest of the sky in Pale Blue, blending it with the Pale Orange.

4. Using rounded strokes, paint the underside of the clouds in Grey and the tops of the clouds in White.

MOUNTAINS

1. Study the finished painting. Note that the mountains should look hazy.

2. Using light strokes, paint the left side of each mountain in Purple.

3. Paint the right side of each mountain in Light Purple.

4. Lightly add a little Pale Orange to the Light Purple and add a few strokes in between the mountains.

TREES

1. Study the finished painting. Notice that the trees can be painted in 3 'sections', using the boats as dividing lines.

2. Paint the base of the left section of trees in the dark tone (Deep Green). Paint the top of this section in the medium tone (Green). Use half-circular strokes which suggest trees of varying heights.

3. Paint the base of the middle section of trees in the medium tone (Green). Paint the top of this section in the light tone (Yellow Green).

4. Paint the 2 remaining sections of trees with the light tone (Yellow Green) at the base and Lemon Yellow on the top.

5. Add a line of Purple along the shoreline underneath the trees. Soften it with a touch of Pale Blue.

LAKE COMO

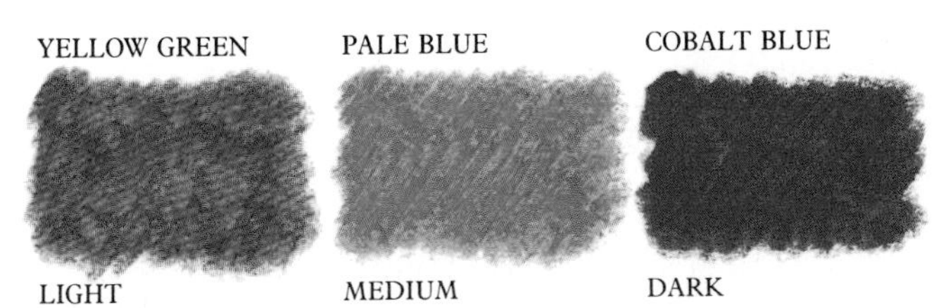

1. Study the finished painting. This is not easy – the aim is to make the lake look full of reflections and shimmering light!

2. Paint a strip of dark tone (Cobalt Blue) underneath the trees.

3. Paint an area of dark tone (Cobalt Blue) underneath the left side of the left mountain as shadow. Then, using horizontal strokes, paint the dark tone (Cobalt Blue) down the left side of the lake, across the bottom and up the right side to the trees.

4. Paint the medium tone (Pale Blue) over the entire lake in long horizontal strokes.

5. Using short, horizontal strokes paint a strip of dark tone (Cobalt Blue) just to the left of the larger boat. Take the strip from the shoreline to the bottom of the lake. Paint a similar strip between the two boats and again to the right of the smaller boat.

6. Using White, paint two long reflections under each boat as shown. Paint similar reflections on the right and left sides of the lake.

7. Using long strokes paint reflections in the light tone (Yellow Green) on the left side of the lake and on the right side under the trees. Also paint long strokes of Yellow Green across the bottom of the lake.

8. Paint a few strokes of the dark tone (Cobalt Blue) between the two reflections of each boat.

9. Add further horizontal strokes of White and Yellow Green over the whole of the lake. Accent with Light Purple underneath the boats, where the mountains form a shadow on the water and over the surface of the lake as shown.

BOATS

1. Study the finished painting. Note that the sails lean slightly to the right and that they look full of movement. You do not need to paint a mast between the sails.

2. Paint the boats in Van Dyke Brown with a touch of Orange as highlight. Make the boats long and delicate in shape. Add tiny strokes of Purple to suggest people on board.

3. Paint the sails in White, highlighted with Pale Orange and Yellow Green. Use White to paint a suggestion of a bow wave under the boats.

White Birches

1. Use sandpaper 23×30cm (9×12in) placed horizontally.

2. Study the painting and drawings on pages 56 and 57 carefully.

3. Draw the grid lines in pencil and then, also in pencil, sketch in the simplified picture as shown opposite above.

4. The light is coming from the left (note the shadows on the right side of the trees) so lightly shade in these areas in pencil.

5. Take the purple pastel pencil and outline the objects and paint in the shadow lightly as shown opposite below. Don't outline the top branches of the trees, you will paint the sky first and add the branches later (see second drawing).

6. Erase all the grid lines, the small trees and the top branches of the birches, leaving the purple outline intact (see opposite below).

THE DRAWING

THE PAINTING

SKY

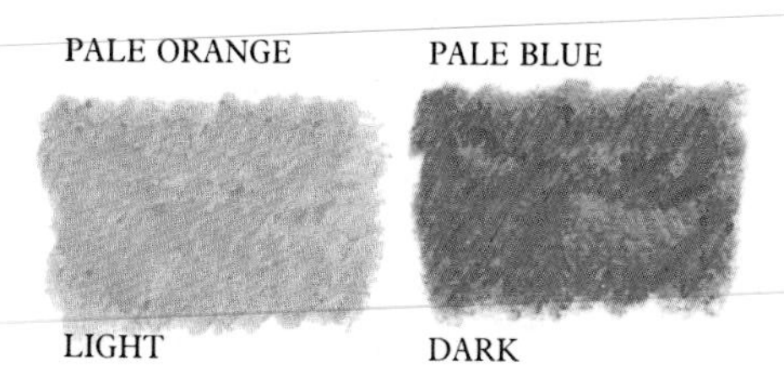

1. Study the finished painting.

2. Using upward, slanting strokes paint Pale Orange along the tops of the mountains.

3. Paint Pale Blue over the rest of the sky, blending it with the Pale Orange.

MOUNTAINS

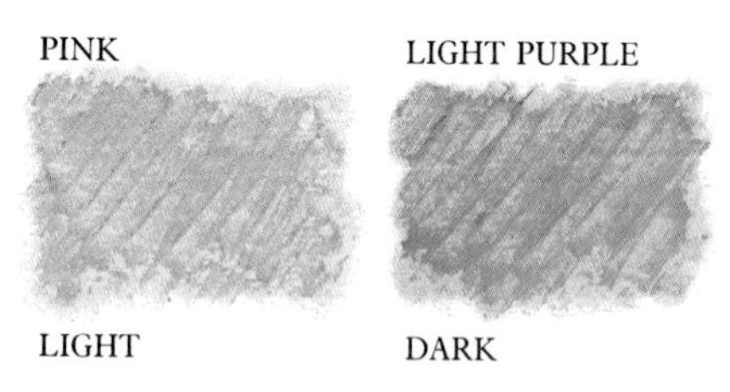

1. Study the finished painting. Note that the mountains behind the trees are closer than the others and darker in tone.

2. Paint the right side of the mountains on the right in Light Purple and the left side in Pink.

3. Paint the mountains behind the trees in Purple as shown.

4. With purple pastel pencil draw in the branches which you erased earlier.

BACKGROUND HILLS AND ROAD

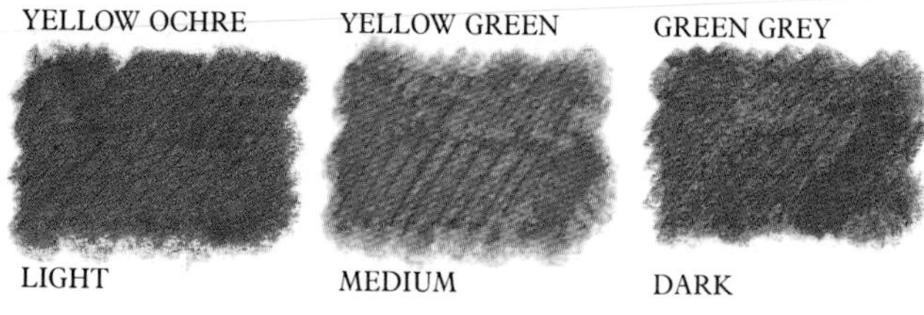

1. Study the finished painting. Note that there are two hills either side of the curving road.

2. Paint the right side of the hill on the right in the dark tone (Green Grey). Shade the left side up to the road in the medium tone (Yellow Green).

3. Paint the right side of the hill on the left in the dark tone (Green Grey). Shade a little of the right side in the light tone (Yellow Ochre) also.

4. Paint the rest of the hill in the light tone (Yellow Ochre). Take the colour right through the vegetation behind the birches – you can paint these in later.

5. Paint the road in Yellow Ochre and stroke Pale Orange around the top curve.

FOREGROUND HILLS

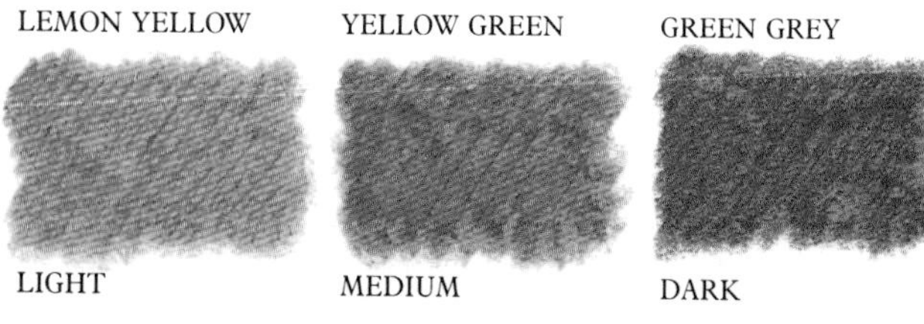

1. Study the finished painting. Note that the ground beneath the trees is in distinct shadow. Try to give the impression of uneven grassy terrain.

2. Paint the right side of the foreground with the dark tone (Green Grey). Shade the area towards the trees in the medium tone (Yellow Green).

3. Stroke Purple over the Green Grey but be careful not to lose the Green Grey completely.

4. Paint alternate strokes of Lemon Yellow and Yellow Ochre over the Yellow Green.

5. Paint the area around the trees in the dark tone (Green Grey) and paint Purple over it. Add strokes of Brown as well as shown. Make sure your strokes slope to the left.

6. Paint dark shadows behind each tree with Purple and Prussian Blue. Stroke a little Pale Blue over the whole of the foreground as shown.

SMALL BACKGROUND TREES

1. Study the finished painting. Note that the trees are of different heights.

2. Using Brown and Purple paint a dark shadow at the base of the line of small trees.

3. Paint the foliage of the trees with Green Grey. Keep the leaves soft and hazy.

4. Paint an impression of brush and also the small tree on the right with Brown. Outline the brush and small tree here and there with black charcoal pencil as shown.

BIRCHES

1. Study the finished painting. Note that the trees are slender and graceful – don't line them up like soldiers! Note also that the foliage should be lacy and soft.

2. Paint the trunks and some branches with Grey. Highlight the trunks with Pale Orange as shown. Outline the right side of the trunk and some of the branches with black charcoal pencil. Add a little Pale Blue as a further highlight.

3. Use the same technique for painting the trees as you used in *Summertime*. Refer to the step-by-step illustration on page 22 if necessary. Paint the dark tone (Deep Green) on the right of the trees and across the branches. Add a little Purple over this.

4. Stroke the medium tone (Green) on the left of the tree and over the Deep Green. Then add the light tone (Yellow Green) on top. Highlight the leaves here and there with Pale Orange and Pale Blue as shown.

Fruit and Flowers

1. Use sandpaper 30×35cm (12×14in) placed horizontally.

2. Study the drawings and painting on pages 60 and 61 carefully.

3. Draw the grid lines in pencil and then, also in pencil, sketch in the simplified picture as shown opposite above. You can place the blue vase more easily if you draw a box around it as shown in the second drawing.

4. The light is coming from the left (note the shadows on the right of the objects) so lightly shade in these areas in pencil.

5. Take the purple pastel pencil and outline the objects and paint in the shadow lightly as shown opposite below.

6. Erase all the grid lines, leaving the purple outline intact (see opposite below).

THE PAINTING

BACKGROUND

1. Study the finished painting. Note that the sandpaper forms the major part of the background.

2. With the flat side of the Yellow Ochre pastel paint long vertical strokes over the background as far as the table.

3. With the flat side of the Orange pastel paint long vertical strokes lightly over the Yellow Ochre. You will, of course, have to remove the paper wrapper if you have not already done so.

4. With the flat side of the Purple pastel paint in an impression of a table using horizontal strokes. Also paint in the shadows – these are mostly on the right side of the orange, the bowl and vase and under the single flower. Stroke a few Purple vertical lines under all the objects as shown.

BLUE VASE

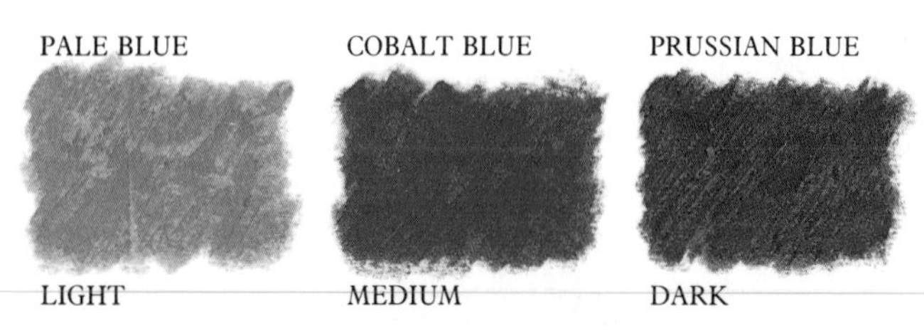

1. Study the finished painting. Note that you should keep your strokes slightly rounded to achieve the rounded form of the vase.

2. Paint the right side of the vase in the dark tone (Prussian Blue). Paint the ridge at the very bottom of the vase and the area above it in the Prussian Blue also. Paint a little of the medium tone (Cobalt Blue) on the left side of the vase.

3. Paint the medium tone (Cobalt Blue) in the middle of the vase and the light tone (Pale Blue) on the left side.

4. Add a little medium tone (Cobalt Blue) to the Pale Blue on the extreme left of the vase but be careful not to lose the Pale Blue completely.

5. Add a little Yellow Green to the Pale Blue on the left of the vase.

6. Paint White highlights on the vase as shown. Press down hard on the pastel for a strong colour.

WHITE BOWL

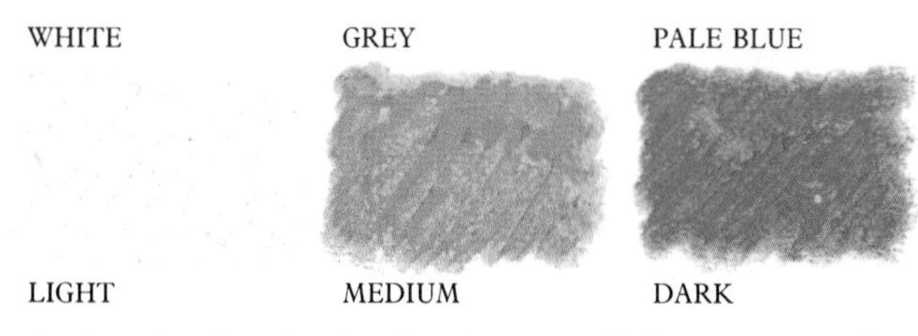

1. Study the finished painting. Make your strokes rounded once again.

2. Paint the right side of the bowl, including the right side of the ridge, in the medium tone (Grey). Stroke the dark tone (Pale Blue) under the lip of the bowl, along the right side, across the bottom and on the ridge. Do not entirely cover the Grey on the ridge.

3. Paint the rest of the bowl and ridge in the light tone (White).

4. Paint the right of the lip in the medium tone (Grey) and the left in White.

YELLOW DAISIES

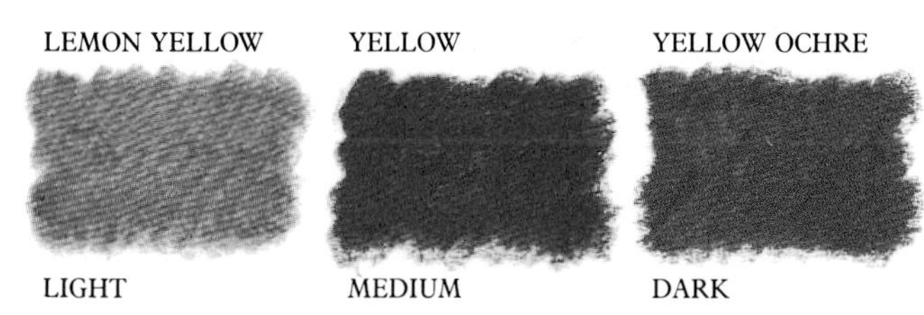

1. Study the finished painting. Note that all the yellow daisies are painted in the same way except for those in profile.

2. Paint the petals on the left in the dark tone (Yellow Ochre). Paint Orange over them as shown.

3. Paint the petals on the right in the medium tone (Yellow). Tip the petals with the light tone (Lemon Yellow).

4. Paint the centres with Brown on the right side and Orange on the left. Add a highlight of Lemon Yellow. Outline the right side of the centres in the purple pastel pencil.

5. Paint the right side of the profile daisy on the right with the dark tone (Yellow Ochre). Paint the overlapping petals with the medium tone (Yellow) as shown.

6. Paint the right side of the profile daisy at the top in the dark tone (Yellow Ochre). Paint the left petals in the medium tone (Yellow). The centre is Brown and Orange.

WHITE DAISIES

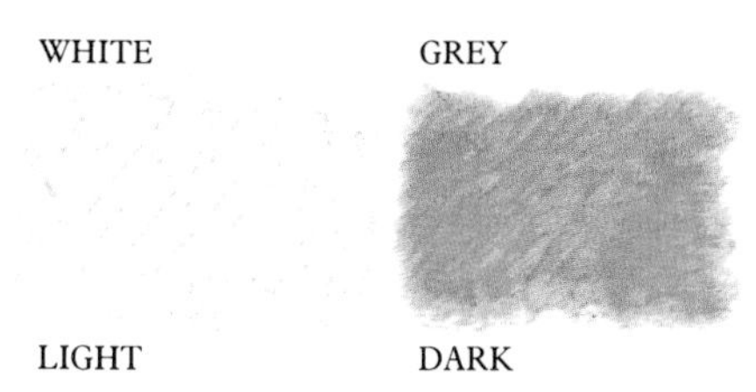

1. Study the finished painting. Note that all the white daisies are painted in the same way except for those in profile.

2. Paint the petals on the left in Grey. Tip them with White.

3. Paint the petals on the right in White.

4. Paint the centres with Brown on the right side and Orange on the left. Add a highlight of Lemon Yellow. Outline the right side of the centres in the purple pastel pencil.

5. Paint the right side of the profile daisies with Grey. Paint the overlapping petals in White.

6. Carefully stroke Purple between the flowers and into the edges of the petals as shown.

LEAVES

1. Use the dark and medium tones (Deep Green and Green) to paint the leaves extending from the flowers as shown. Keep the leaves delicate and lacy. Add the light tone (Yellow Green) to the leaves on the left. Paint touches of Pale Blue here and there between the flowers.

APPLE

1. Study the finished painting.

2. Paint the right side and bottom of the apple and the left side of the stem area with Green Grey. Keep your strokes rounded.

3. Paint the rest of the apple and the right side of the stem area in Yellow Green. Paint the stem with the purple pastel pencil. Add a White highlight as shown.

ORANGES

1. Study the finished picture.

2. Paint the top of the orange in the bowl in the light tone (Yellow Orange) and the rest of it in the medium tone (Orange). Add a tiny White highlight as shown.

3. Paint the right side of the orange on the table with the dark tone (Vermilion), shading to the medium and light tones (Orange and Yellow Orange) at the top. Paint a small dot of Purple on the stem and also a White highlight as shown.

PEAR

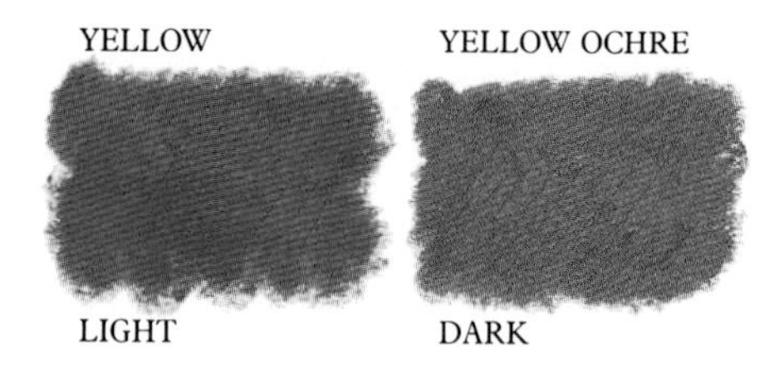

1. Study the finished painting.

2. Paint the right side of the pear in Yellow Ochre and the left side in Yellow. Add a touch of Orange to the Yellow Ochre. Paint a White highlight at the top and bottom of the pear as shown.

GRAPES

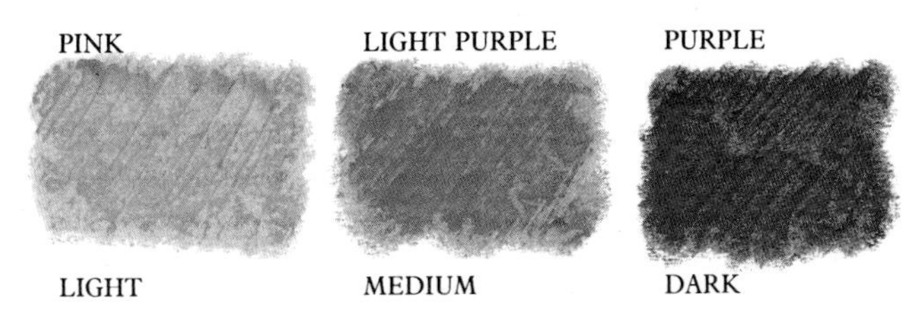

1. Study the finished painting and the step-by-step illustration.

2. Paint a line of Purple around the bunch of grapes where they rest on the other fruit in the bowl.

3. Outline the grapes again with the purple pastel pencil.

4. Paint the right side of the grapes in the dark tone (Purple) and the left side in the medium tone (Light Purple) – see the first and second steps.

5. Add a little light tone (Pink) to the Light Purple, but be careful not to lose the colour completely. Add a touch of Pale Blue to the Purple. Paint a dot of White in the middle of each grape as a highlight – see the third step.

6. Stroke the Pale Blue here and there around the other fruit for accent.

7. Paint the stem of the fallen flower with Deep Green and touches of Yellow Green as shown. The flower is painted in Orange and Yellow Orange.

8. Paint a few vertical strokes of Pale Blue under the blue vase and similar strokes of White under the white bowl. These are reflections.

This is the most ambitious painting in the book but I'm sure you will be very pleased with the finished result – and with all the other paintings you have done. You will now have the confidence to paint on your own, using this book for guidance and inspiration. Happy Painting!

PAINTING
IN OILS

For all the paintings in this book Nancy Kominsky has used Rowney Georgian Oil Colours which she has found to be the most suitable for her purposes. They are permanent and their consistency is incomparable for palette knife painting.

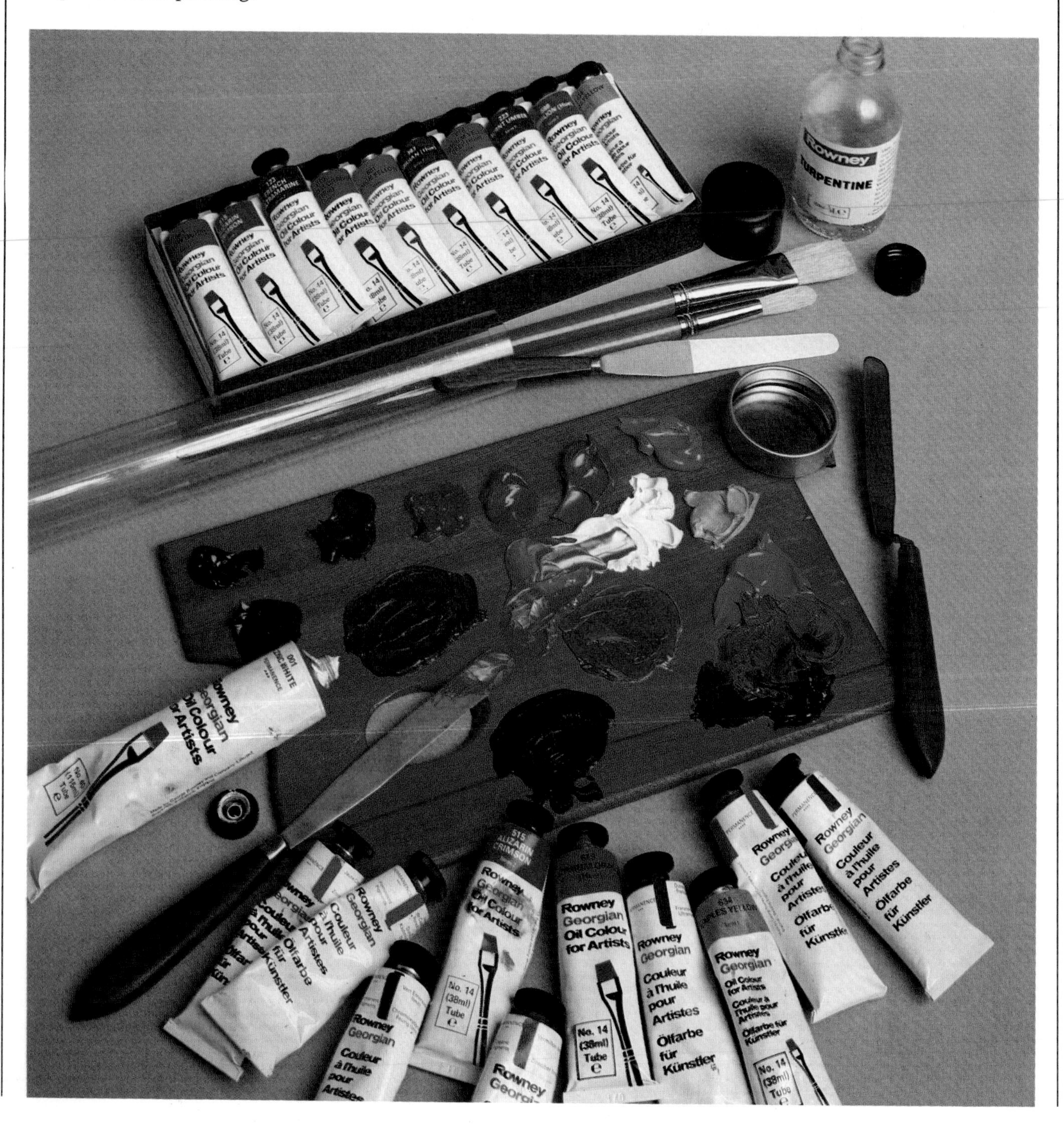

Before you paint

PAINTING MATERIALS

The following is a list of colours and other required painting materials.

1. Paints

The names of the colours used in this list of oil paints are universal ones and apply to most manufacturers throughout the world. The best size to buy is the 4-inch No. 14 (38 ml) tube of oil paint. Keep to the same colours as those recommended or else your colour mixes will vary from the mixing guides shown in this book.

Lemon Yellow
Cadmium Yellow Deep
Naples Yellow
Yellow Ochre
Cadmium Orange
Alizarin Crimson
Vermilion
Viridian (green)
Burnt Umber
French Ultramarine (blue)
Extra large tube of Zinc or Flake White,
the 6-inch No. 40 (115 ml) size

Almost twice as much white is needed because it is used in the mixing of every colour, especially the light tones and objects such as sky, water or snow. There is very little difference between Zinc and Flake White. Zinc White, however, does not dry as rapidly and is easier to use in mixing colour. Both Zinc and Flake White are universal names.

2. Palette knives

(a) *Offset knife:* this is the same as the painting knife. The small elevation at the base of the handle keeps the fingers out of the paint while in use. In painting the offset knife is held lightly and the paint stroked on usually with the flat of the knife.

How to hold an offset knife

(b) *Straight knife:* this is used for mixing colours. The mixture of paint is simply turned over and over while mixing but make sure that the pile of paint is kept contained and doesn't spread all over the palette.

3. Brushes

(a) If you are painting with a knife you will also need the following brushes:

- One No. 12 or No. 10 – a flat, hog bristle brush. This is used for the umber wash.
- One No. 8 or No. 6 – a medium, round, hog bristle brush. This is used for the drawing.

(b) If you are painting with a brush rather than with a knife, you will need the same brushes as mentioned above as well as the following:

- One No. 2 or No. 4 – a flat, hog bristle brush.
- One No. 2 or No. 4 – a round, sable brush.

In brush painting, the smaller-size sable brushes are best. As you progress, you will probably want to add more brushes to your range.

4. Turpentine

This is used not only for the umber wash and the drawing, but also for cleaning the palette, brushes and one's fingers. White spirit or kerosene can also be used if you do not like the smell of turpentine – these solvents are practically odourless.

5. Palette

A large square wooden palette, approximately 12 by 16 inches (30 by 41 cm) is the best. (You can also buy large tear-off palette pads which have the advantage of being disposable after each painting.) A wooden palette of this size, especially with the paint on it, is too heavy to hold and so it doesn't matter if you are right or left handed. Simply place the palette on a flat surface to the right or to the left of the easel. If you are painting with a knife you need both hands free to be able to keep on cleaning the knife as you paint.

6. Single-tin dipper

A large single-tin dipper is needed to hold the turpentine.

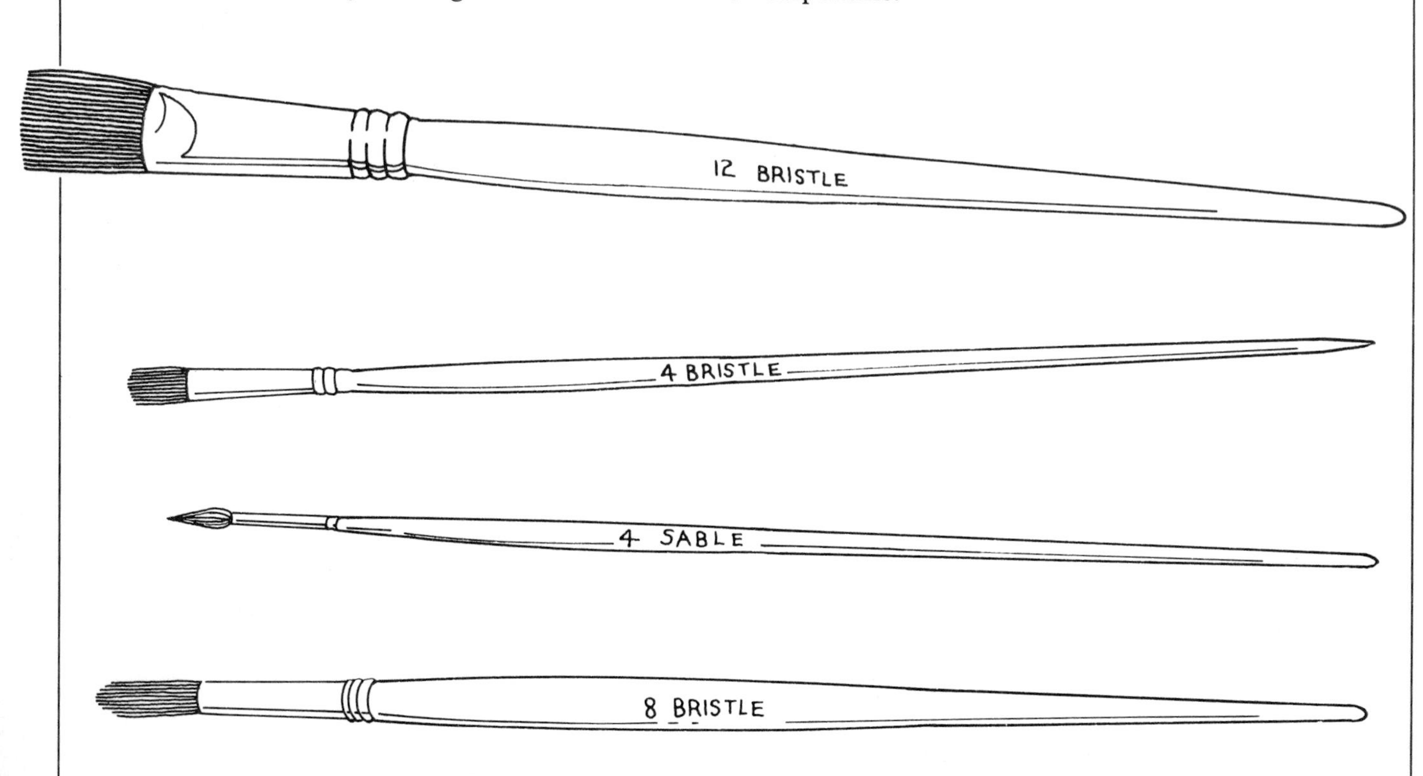

A selection of brushes used for painting

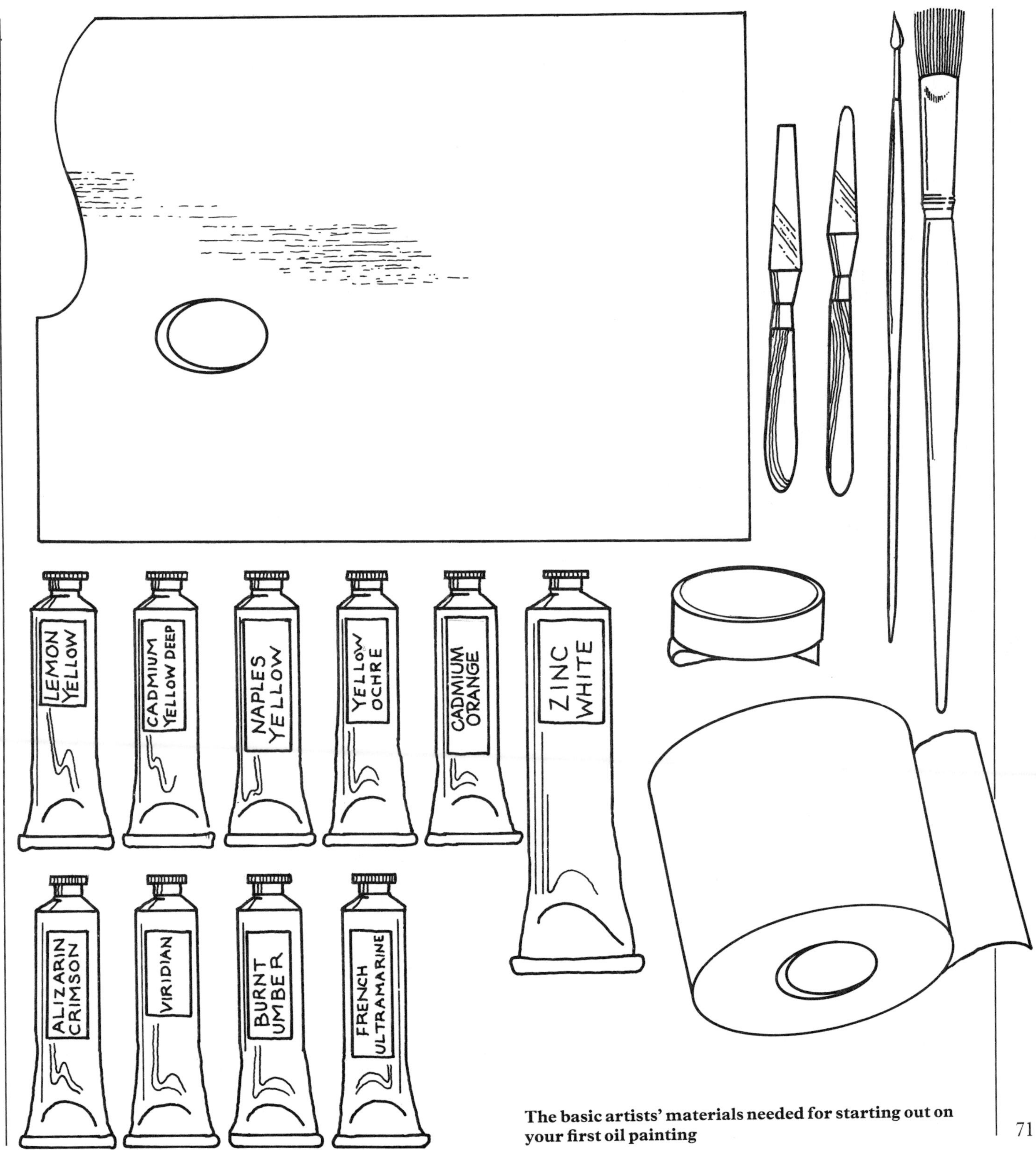

The basic artists' materials needed for starting out on your first oil painting

7. Toilet tissue
This is cheaper than cotton rag and has the advantage of being disposable. It is used to wipe the excess moisture from the umber wash and to wipe out mistakes in the drawing. It is also essential for cleaning the knife during painting and to clean the palette after scraping off the paint.

8. A plastic litter bag

9. Canvas or canvas boards
Use any one of the following, 14 by 18 inches (36 by 46 cm).

(a) *Stretched canvas:* until you are more experienced, buy cotton canvas which has already been stretched. Do not buy primed canvas as this is very expensive. A beginner to oil painting should not attempt to stretch his own canvas as a badly stretched canvas will result in ripples on the surface. You will also need to buy a special tool and stretcher frames amongst other things.

(b) *Canvas board:* this is excellent for a beginner as it is inexpensive.

(c) *Hardboard:* this is the least expensive material, especially for very large paintings. The texture is interesting and it can be bought at any timber merchant. Use the rough side of the board. If painting with a brush, cover the board with several coats of household undercoat paint (acrylic emulsion). If using a knife to paint with, it is probably not necessary to undercoat, in which case you can draw straight onto the hardboard with chalk.

10. Easel
Use whatever is available but make sure that it is sturdy. A table easel is very useful if you are short of storage space as not only does it fold away but the table on which you place the easel provides a good surface on which to put all your painting equipment, such as palette and knives.

11. Cling film or tin foil
Use either of these to cover any leftover paint on the palette. If you put the palette in the fridge the paint will keep indefinitely. You can also put any piles of leftover mixed paint in a tin foil dish, cover and put in your freezer.

12. Artists' clear picture varnish
Six months after the painting is completed, dust it off with a soft, dry brush. Apply the clear varnish lightly with a large, flat brush. Lay the painting flat until it is dry. This is to avoid 'tears' of varnish running down the canvas. The varnish will take about an hour to dry.

13. Where to paint
The ideal place to paint is in a north-facing room but most people make do with a corner of any room that is spare and use electric rather than natural light. Natural light is preferable, but the important thing is to have space to move about in and to be comfortable. After all, painting is supposed to be enjoyable.

A selection of easels

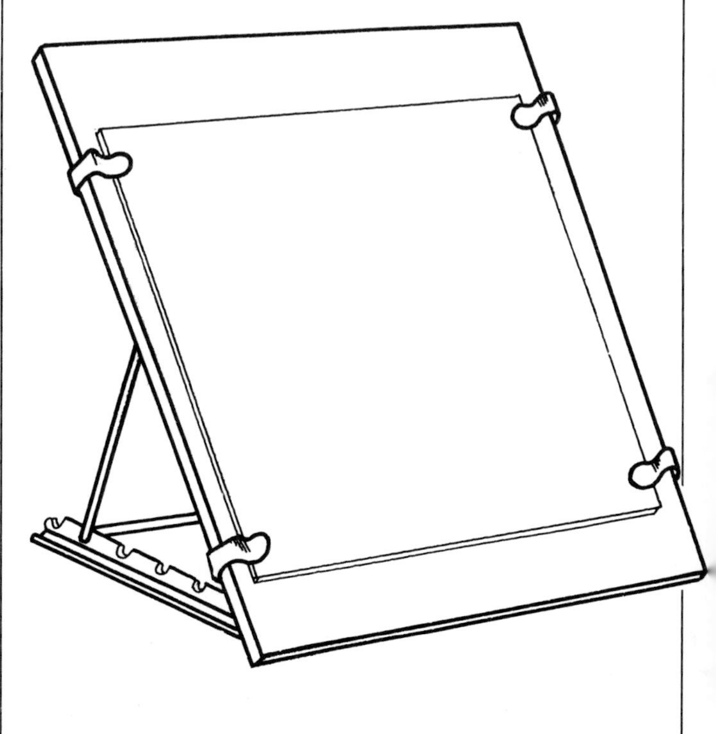

Table easel

Studio easel
Folding easel

MEASUREMENTS FOR MIXING THE COLOURS

1. In an oil painting, colour is the most important thing to consider, far more than the drawing. In the colour mixing guide, I have broken down each mixture into precise amounts of colour needed, just like the ingredients of a cookery recipe. For measuring out the different quantities of paint, I have used the idea of spoons. Don't actually measure the paint out onto the palette with spoons but use the drawings below to judge how much paint you need to squeeze from the tube.

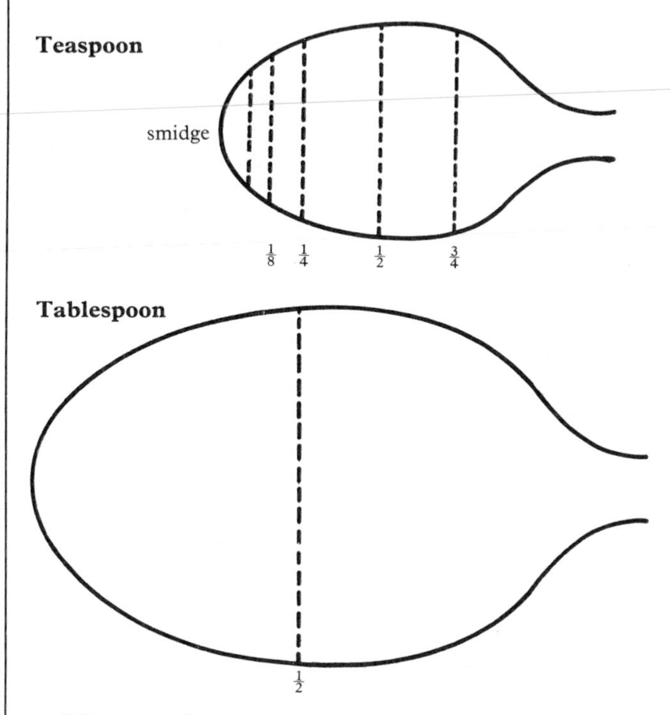

These different amounts apply mostly to knife painting as this uses up more paint. The exact quantities for mixing a colour ensure that you have sufficient for each area of the painting. You can end up using just as much paint by mixing bits here and there which is a time-consuming nuisance.

2. Always try to keep your pile of mixed paint clean. If you have any mixed paint left over when you have finished painting, remove it from the mixing area and place it neatly at the edge of the palette.

3. Next, clean the mixing area before mixing another colour. To do this, scrape the mixing area with a straight knife and wipe it clean with turpentine or another solvent and toilet tissue. The mixing area must be left clean after each session.

1. Before applying the oil paint to the canvas, you must cover it with an umber wash. This is called underpainting and gives the finished painting a richer colour. The damp canvas also allows you to wipe off any mistakes in the drawing with toilet tissue as you go along.

To make the umber wash, squeeze out ½ teaspoonful of Burnt Umber onto the mixing area of the palette. Dip the large, flat, bristle brush into the turpentine, making sure that it does not drip, and then dip the brush into the Burnt Umber on the palette, pulling some aside with the brush to make a light, rather thin wash.

Cover the canvas with the umber wash but take care not to make it too dark or too runny. Wipe off any excess moisture with toilet tissue but leave the canvas damp.

2. To divide the canvas up into sections, use the medium round brush and umber wash. Use slightly more Burnt Umber than turpentine this time in order to achieve a darker colour wash.

If your canvas is to be used vertically, draw three vertical lines equally spaced and five horizontal lines. If the canvas is to be used horizontally, draw five equally spaced vertical lines and three horizontal lines. When doing this, a useful tip is to divide the canvas into quarters first, then divide each section as indicated. If your canvas is square, draw three equally spaced vertical lines and three equally spaced horizontal lines. The sections do not have to be measured exactly. This method of sectioning-off the canvas can be used for any size canvas. In a larger canvas, the squares will be larger but so will the scale of the drawing.

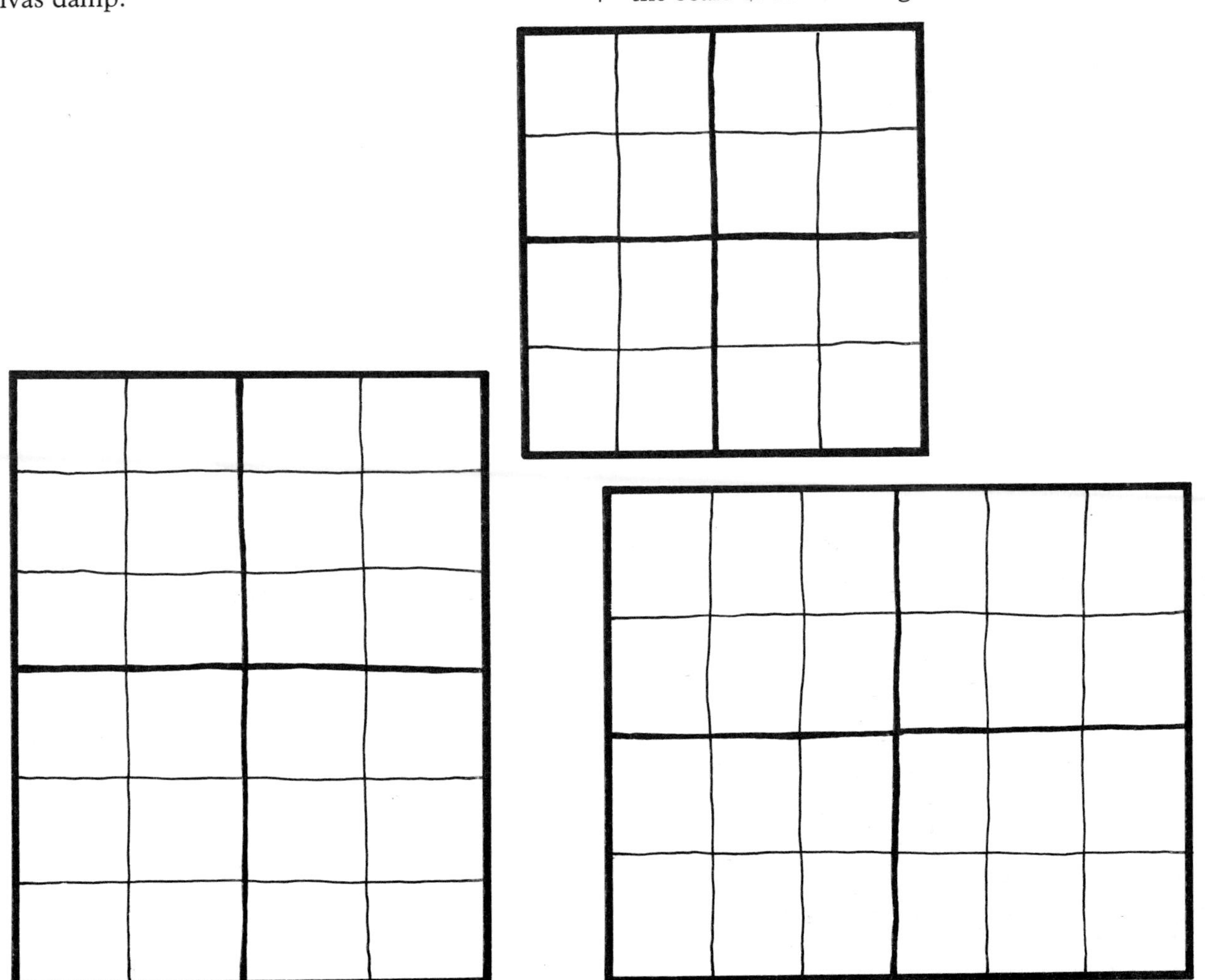

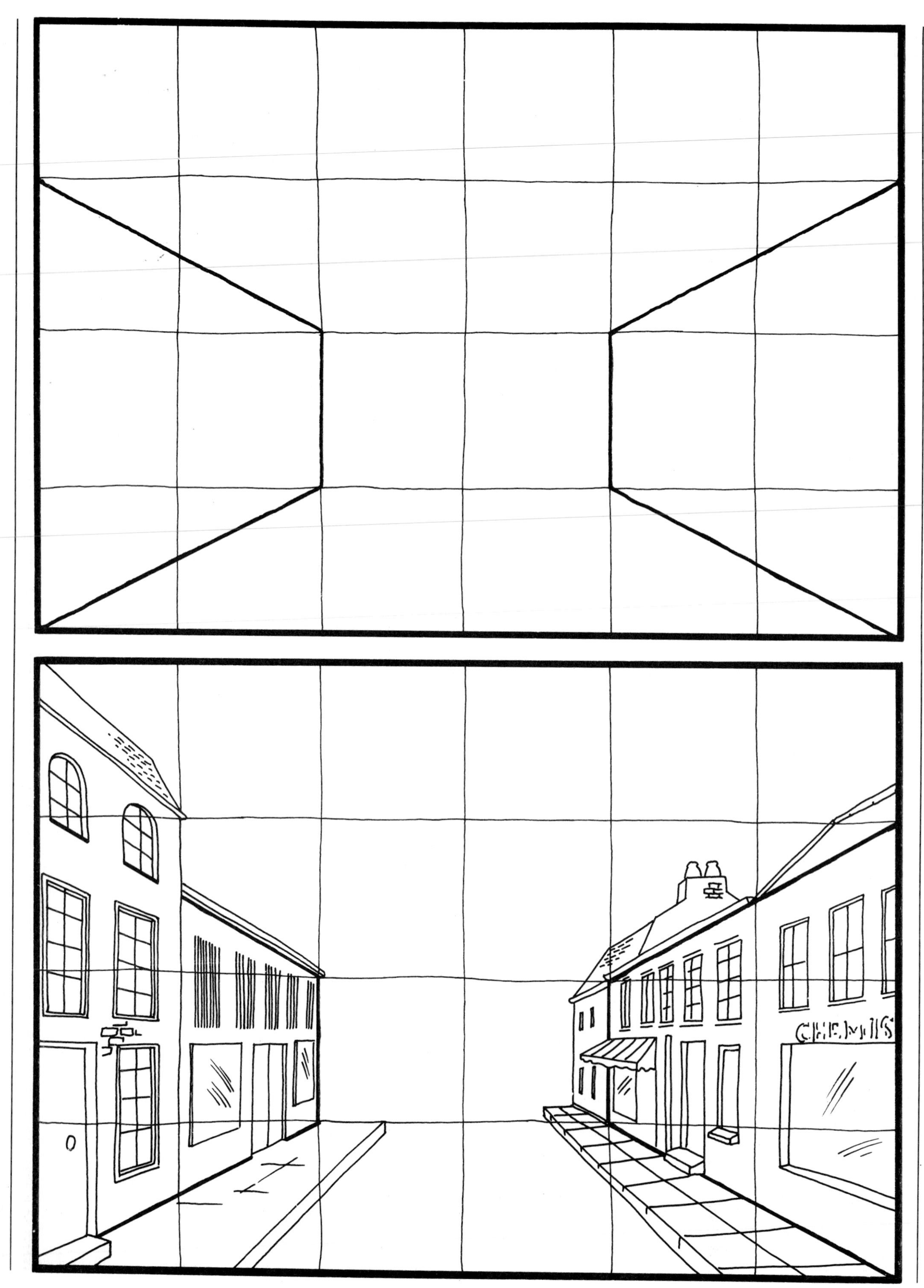
CHEMIS

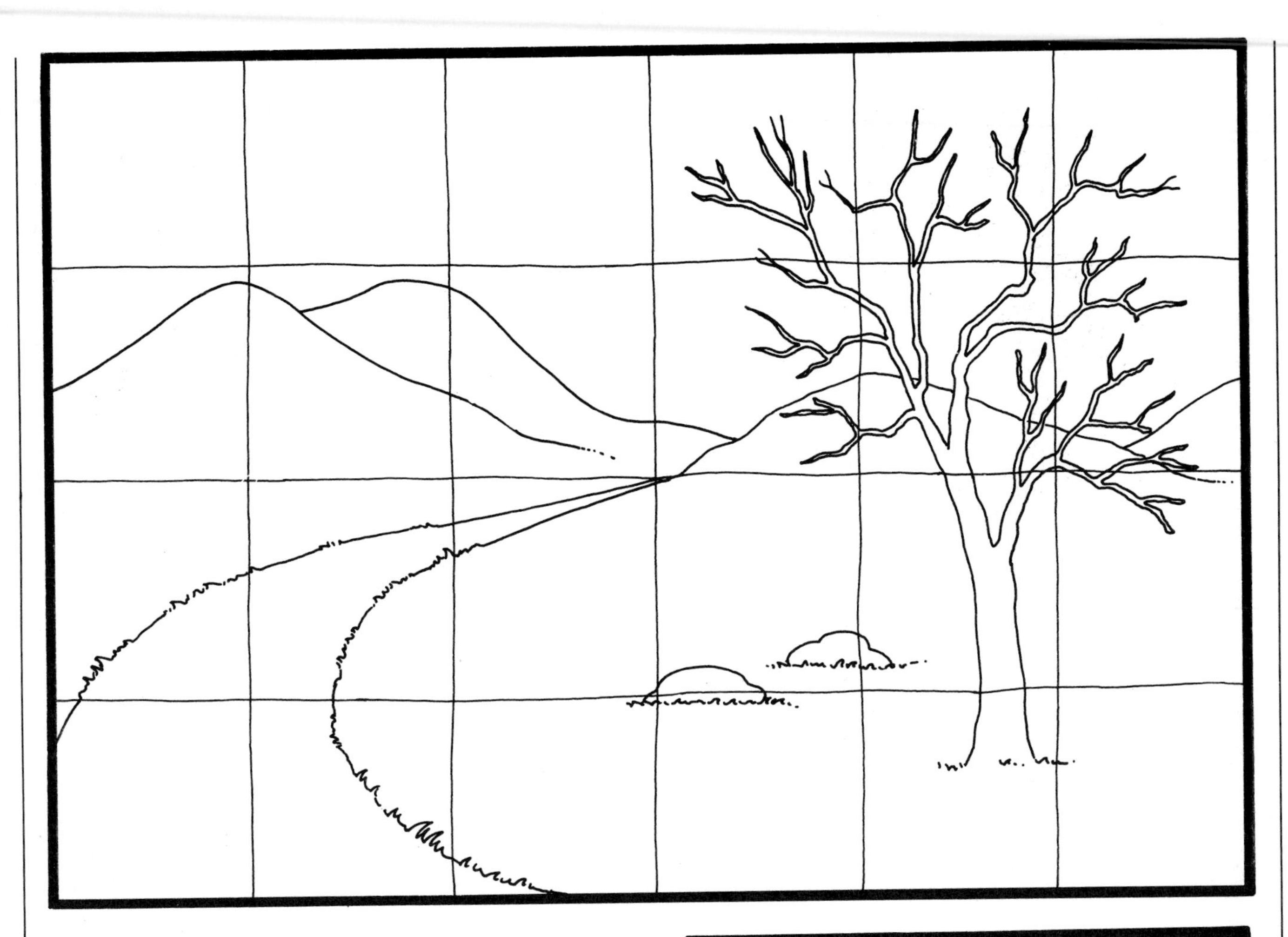

3. In placing work on the canvas, start at the bottom and mark a place for the objects before drawing them in. This helps with correct placement and sizing. Use the squares as guidelines, they are invaluable in street scenes and anywhere else where perspective is used. Put objects, such as vases, in a box, again using the squares as guidelines, to make sure that both sides are equal.

4. Put in the rough drawing with the medium round brush and umber wash. Ignore any detail of the subject matter for the time being: do not put petals on flowers yet, nor leaves on trees and rigging on boats. The details will be painted in later.

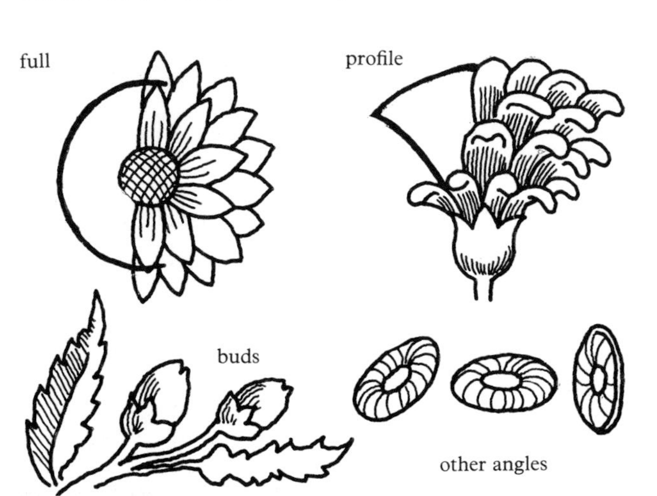

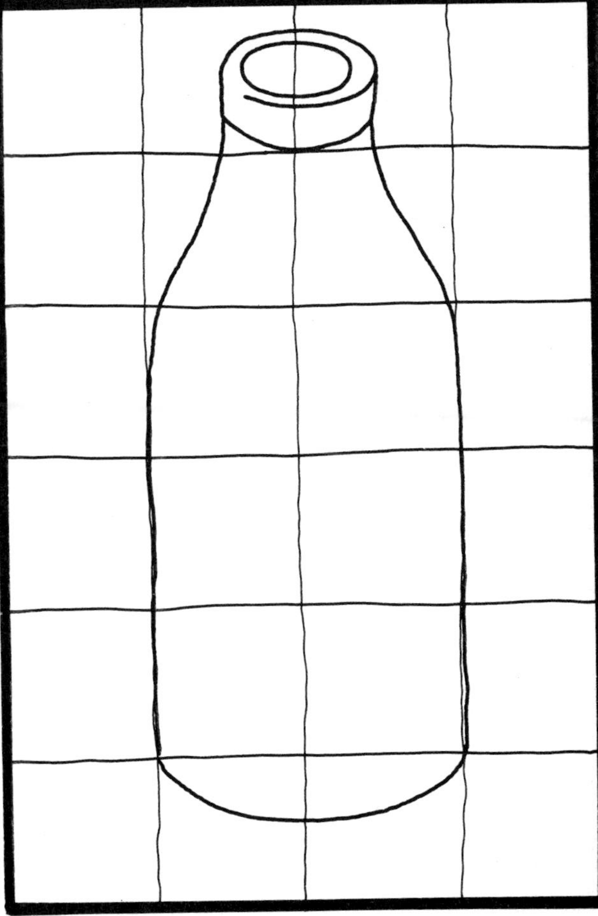

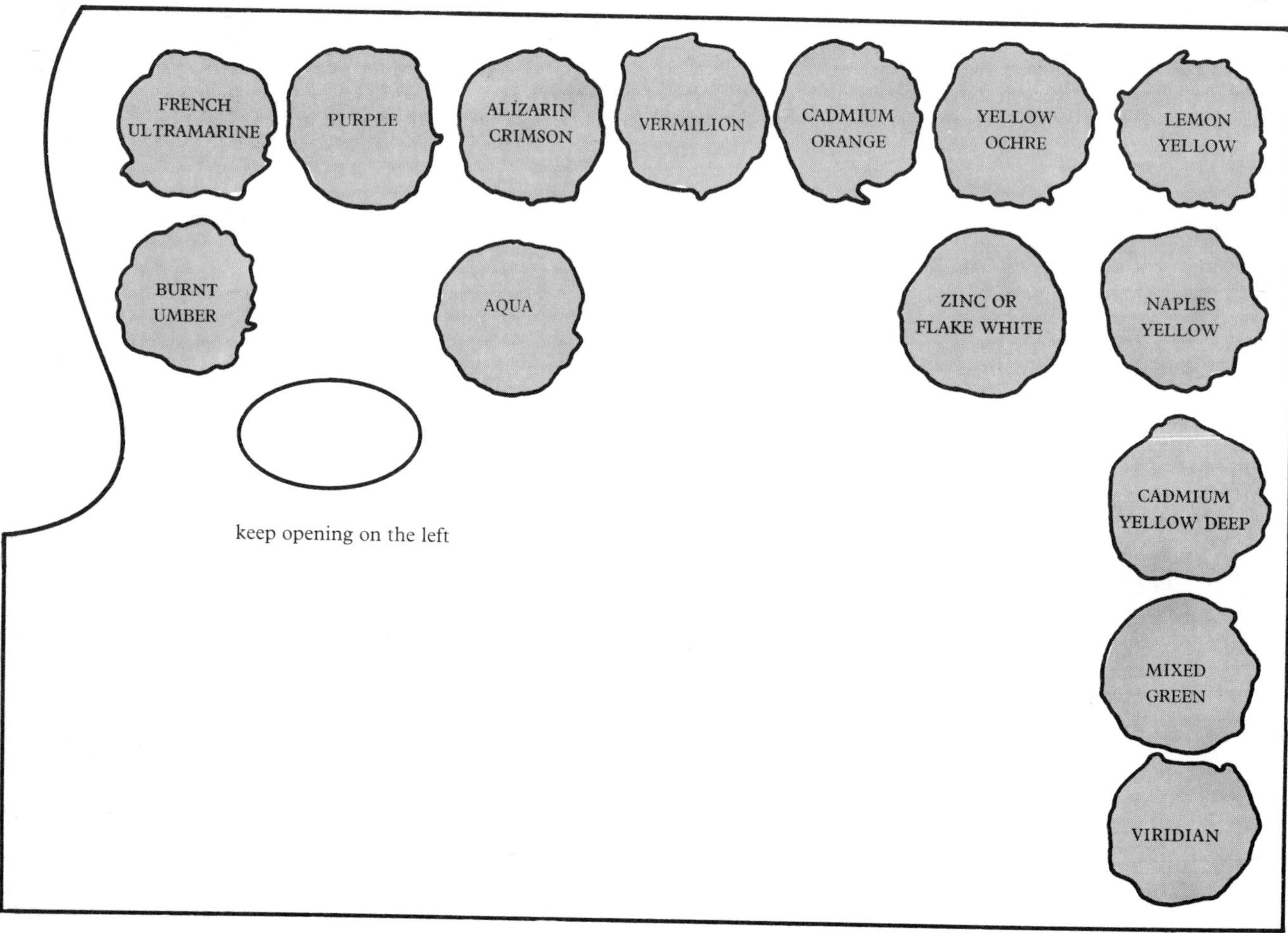
FRENCH ULTRAMARINE
PURPLE
ALIZARIN CRIMSON
VERMILION
CADMIUM ORANGE
YELLOW OCHRE
LEMON YELLOW
BURNT UMBER
AQUA
ZINC OR FLAKE WHITE
NAPLES YELLOW
CADMIUM YELLOW DEEP
MIXED GREEN
VIRIDIAN
keep opening on the left

5. The most important thing, before mixing the colour, is to decide where the light is coming from in a painting and then to loosely add shading where the shadows will be. Continue to be conscious of light and shadow until the last stroke has been added. The light usually falls from one particular side. If in doubt, check the shadows on your subject – if they are on the left, the light is coming from the righthand side and vice versa.

6. Set up your palette as shown in the drawing opposite, squeezing out about a teaspoonful of each colour. The colour mixtures of aqua, purple and mixed green should be made up as indicated below.

(a) *Aqua:* mix together $\frac{1}{2}$ teaspoonful Viridian and 1 teaspoonful Zinc or Flake White.
(b) *Purple:* mix together $\frac{1}{2}$ teaspoonful Alizarin Crimson and $\frac{1}{2}$ teaspoonful French Ultramarine.
(c) *Mixed green:* mix together 1 teaspoonful Cadmium Yellow and $\frac{1}{2}$ teaspoonful Viridian.

7. The paint should be laid out on the palette in the same order each time so that it soon becomes easy to find the right colour. The order of colour shown on the palette works for both right- and left-handed people.

8. Be accurate when mixing your colours. You may find that your colour mixes vary slightly from the colour swatches shown in this book but this is due to the limitations of colour printing. Just make sure you keep the tonal values correct, such as keeping the extra light lighter than the light tone.

9. Keep your paint on the palette clean while working by cleaning your knife with turpentine before going from one colour to the next.

10. Always use a straight knife for mixing paint. Using a brush will ruin it and makes the brush too thick to give clean strokes.

Facing page: the order of paints on the palette

How to create the effect of mountains using the flat of the offset knife

The flat of the offset knife can also be used for painting leaves and flowers

11. If you are painting with a brush, just pick up the paint on the brush, apply to the canvas and stroke it on in the form of the object being painted – for example, use round strokes for round objects. The drawings above show how the shape of the strokes affects the final painting. Don't just fill in empty spaces. You are creating a form. Always be conscious of the shape of the object you are painting. This applies also to the application of paint with the palette knife.

TONAL VALUES

The following are the basic cool and warm colours: (This does not refer to tints derived from these colours.)

Warm: yellow, red and orange
Cool: blue, green and purple
Primary colours: blue, red and yellow

You can make all other colours from primary colours. For example, blue and yellow make green. Cool colours tend to grey or cool the warm colours and vice versa. Use the complementary or greying colour sparingly.

Warm colours advance into the foreground of a painting and are more intense. Cool colours recede into the background and become cooler and paler with bluish and purple overtones.

BASICS FOR MIXING COLOURS

1. Each area on the canvas (background, objects etc) is broken down into at least three tonal values: light, medium and dark. As you become more experienced, two additional tones or more are added in polishing the painting, including the brightest highlight and accenting the shadow.

2. The medium, or mother colour (the general colour of the object) is mixed first.

3. Divide the medium colour into three piles – one small ($\frac{1}{2}$ teaspoonful) for the light tone and two piles of equal size.

4. To the small or light tone, add twice as much white and nearly always a smidge of Naples Yellow. See each colour mixing guide for specific instructions on which colours need a smidge of Naples Yellow. The touch of yellow prevents the light tone from becoming chalky and lifeless.

5. Do not touch the middle tone.

6. To the dark, or third tone, add purple or another darkening agent – not Burnt Umber. Easy does it. If the original colour of the dark tone is lost or muddied in the mixing by adding too much purple, add some of the colour used for the middle or medium tone. This restores the original colour but retains the dark of the third tone.

7. Do not add purple as a general rule to sky and sea colours.

GETTING STARTED

1. Paint in the dark tones first, followed by the middle tones and then the light tones. Only mix tones where they meet so as not to lose tonal values or muddy the colours. This is very important to preserve the contrast between light and dark in the paintings.

2. The medium and dark colours are used in the shadows of the painting. In the light area, the medium and light tones of colour are used. Again, please remember that colours must blend at the edges where they meet.

3. Work your paintings in the following order:

Landscape and seascape: paint the background or sky first. Always put light tone at the horizon, followed by the middle tone and then the dark tone at the top. Put in the ground colour, trees and other objects last. Use the offset knife for painting in the colour.

Still life: paint in the background first. Next paint in the foreground and then the vase or whatever is the subject of the painting. Lastly add the flowers and details to the vase.

SOME GUIDELINES BEFORE MIXING THE COLOURS

1. Read all the directions carefully. Mix the colours as directed with a straight knife. Remember to keep the knife clean when going from one colour to another.

2. There should be a distinct difference in tonal values. Mix the colours in the order given but don't panic if the colours don't look exactly like the colour swatches in this book. There will be slight variations due to the limitations of colour printing.

3. The colour mixes given are mixed in amounts adequate for a small canvas. A 14 by 18 inch (36 by 46 cm) canvas is an excellent size for beginners and avoids the constant mixing and matching of dabs of paint to cover the canvas.

4. Some areas in a painting will not use up all the paint mixture made up. Do not throw away the paint but transfer the blobs to a shallow tin foil dish, cover lightly with cling film and put in the freezer. It will stay fluid and keep for ever. You can use this extra paint on a smaller canvas later.

5. All highlight used in painting fruits, vegetables, vases and glass is one basic mixture.
Make up the highlight as follows:
$\frac{3}{4}$ teaspoon White
smidge of Naples Yellow
This highlight can also be used for sea foam.

6. All the following colour mixes can be used for objects and areas in any painting, for example:

Tones of white: snow, clouds, vases, flowers, buildings.
Tones of green: foliage, shrubs, grass, vases, trees and vegetables.
Greyed burnt orange: backgrounds, copper, barns, brick, roofs and vases.

After deciding on your subject, you will find that you can use or adapt any colour from the colour mixing guide in this book to suit your particular needs and in exact amounts to take the guesswork out of mixing colour. Use the index to find the right colour.

7. Glass

Painting glass is not as mysterious or difficult as it seems at first. After drawing in the outlines of the clear glass vase, paint in the background colour of the painting, painting between the outlines of the vase, making sure that you keep the outline clear. If there are flowers in the vase, paint in the stems in the vase on the background colour. Outline the glass lightly in purple and add highlights wherever necessary.

The colour mixing guide

BASIC COLOUR COMBINATIONS

Colour mix for sky tones

EXTRA LIGHT

LIGHT

MEDIUM

DARK

MEDIUM TONE
1¼ tablespoons White
¼ teaspoon French Ultramarine
½ teaspoon aqua
smidge Cadmium Orange (easy does it)

Mix the paint and separate it into three parts, one small (½ teaspoon) and two equal parts.

1. LIGHT TONE
Use the first part (½ teaspoon).
Add: 1 teaspoon White
⅛ teaspoon Naples Yellow

2. MEDIUM TONE
Use the second part. Leave it as it is.

3. DARK TONE
Use the third part.
Add: ⅛ teaspoon French Ultramarine
¼ teaspoon aqua
smidge Cadmium Orange
smidge purple

4. EXTRA LIGHT TONE
When this is required, to ½ teaspoon light tone
Add: ½ teaspoon White
smidge Naples Yellow
This is used in all skies at the horizon.

- In order to make a rosy tone for the sky at the horizon, add a smidge of orange to the extra light sky tone. The light and extra light sky tones are mostly painted on the horizon.

Colour mix for stormy sky tones

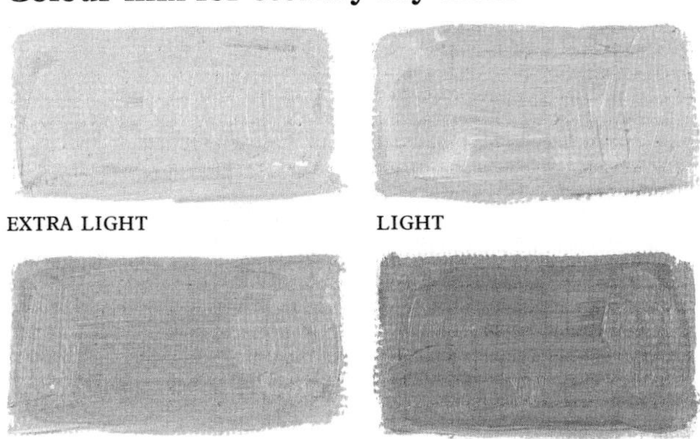

MEDIUM TONE
$1\frac{1}{4}$ tablespoons White
$\frac{1}{4}$ teaspoon French Ultramarine
$\frac{1}{2}$ teaspoon of aqua
$\frac{1}{4}$ teaspoon Cadmium Orange

Mix the paint and separate it into three parts, one small ($\frac{1}{2}$ teaspoon) and two equal parts.

1. LIGHT TONE
Use the first part ($\frac{1}{2}$ teaspoon)
Add: 1 teaspoon White
$\frac{1}{8}$ teaspoon Naples Yellow

2. MEDIUM TONE
Use the second part: leave it as it is.

3. DARK TONE
Use the third part
Add: $\frac{1}{8}$ teaspoon French Ultramarine
$\frac{1}{4}$ teaspoon aqua
smidge Cadmium Orange
smidge purple

4. EXTRA LIGHT TONE
When this is required, to $\frac{1}{2}$ teaspoon light tone
Add: $\frac{1}{2}$ teaspoon White
smidge Naples Yellow

The colours will be greyish. Paint storm clouds with the medium and dark tones.

Colour mix for sky at sundown

MEDIUM TONE
$1\frac{1}{2}$ teaspoons White
$\frac{1}{2}$ teaspoon Yellow Ochre
$\frac{1}{8}$ teaspoon purple
$\frac{1}{4}$ teaspoon Cadmium Orange

Mix the paint and separate it into three parts, one small ($\frac{1}{2}$ teaspoon) and two equal parts.

1. LIGHT TONE
Use the first part ($\frac{1}{2}$ teaspoon)
Add: 1 teaspoon White
$\frac{1}{8}$ teaspoon Naples Yellow
$\frac{1}{8}$ teaspoon Cadmium Orange

2. MEDIUM TONE
Use the second part. Leave it as it is.

3. DARK TONE
Use the third part
Add: $\frac{1}{4}$ teaspoon purple
$\frac{1}{8}$ teaspoon Alizarin Crimson
$\frac{1}{8}$ teaspoon Cadmium Orange

4. EXTRA LIGHT TONE
When this is required, to $\frac{1}{2}$ teaspoon light tone
Add: $\frac{1}{2}$ teaspoon White
smidge Naples Yellow

Colour mix for water and sea tones

EXTRA LIGHT LIGHT

MEDIUM DARK

MEDIUM TONE
$1\frac{1}{4}$ tablespoons White
$\frac{1}{4}$ tablespoon French Ultramarine
$\frac{1}{8}$ teaspoon mixed green
smidge Cadmium Orange (easy does it)

Mix the paint and separate it into three parts, one small ($\frac{1}{2}$ teaspoon) and two equal parts.

1. LIGHT TONE
Use the first part ($\frac{1}{2}$ teaspoon).
Add: 1 teaspoon White
$\frac{1}{8}$ teaspoon Naples Yellow

2. MEDIUM TONE
Use the second part. Leave it as it is.

3. DARK TONE
Use the third part.
Add: $\frac{1}{8}$ teaspoon French Ultramarine
$\frac{1}{4}$ teaspoon aqua
smidge Cadmium Orange
smidge purple

4. EXTRA LIGHT TONE
When this is required, to $\frac{1}{2}$ teaspoon light tone
Add: $\frac{1}{2}$ teaspoon White
smidge Naples Yellow

When painting water, remember that it is the reflection of the sky so water and sea tones are basically sky tones with some green added. Remember that water is shallower nearer the shore and therefore is lighter in colour.

- For sea foam use the following highlight mixture:
$\frac{3}{4}$ teaspoon White
smidge Naples Yellow (easy does it)

Colour mix for earth tones

LIGHT MEDIUM

DARK EXTRA DARK

MEDIUM TONE
1 tablespoon Yellow Ochre
$\frac{1}{2}$ teaspoon White
$\frac{1}{8}$ teaspoon Cadmium Orange

Mix the paint and separate it into three parts, one small ($\frac{1}{2}$ teaspoon) and two equal parts.

1. LIGHT TONE
Use the first part ($\frac{1}{2}$ teaspoon)
Add: $\frac{3}{4}$ teaspoon White
$\frac{1}{2}$ teaspoon Naples Yellow

2. MEDIUM TONE
Use the second part. Leave it as it is.

3. DARK TONE
Use the third part.
Add: $\frac{1}{4}$ teaspoon purple
smidge mixed green

4. EXTRA DARK TONE
When this is required, to $\frac{1}{2}$ teaspoon dark tone
Add: $\frac{1}{8}$ teaspoon purple

Colour mix for tree tones

LIGHT MEDIUM

DARK EXTRA DARK

MEDIUM TONE
$\frac{1}{2}$ teaspoon Burnt Umber
$\frac{1}{2}$ teaspoon Yellow Ochre
$\frac{1}{4}$ teaspoon purple
$\frac{1}{8}$ teaspoon Cadmium Orange

Mix the paint and separate it into three parts, one small ($\frac{1}{2}$ teaspoon) and two equal parts.

1. LIGHT TONE
Use the first part ($\frac{1}{2}$ teaspoon).
Add: $\frac{1}{2}$ teaspoon White
$\frac{1}{4}$ teaspoon Naples Yellow
smidge Cadmium Orange

2. MEDIUM TONE
Use the second part. Leave it as it is.

3. DARK TONE
Use the third part.
Add: $\frac{3}{4}$ teaspoon purple
$\frac{1}{4}$ teaspoon Cadmium Orange

4. EXTRA DARK TONE
When this is required, use purple from the palette. This tone is usually used for slender trees.

The tree tone is used for trees and branches, usually when they are in the foreground.

Colour mix for mountain tones

EXTRA LIGHT LIGHT

MEDIUM DARK

MEDIUM TONE
1 teaspoon White
$\frac{1}{2}$ teaspoon purple
$\frac{1}{8}$ teaspoon Yellow Ochre
smidge mixed green

Mix the paint and separate it into three parts, one small ($\frac{1}{2}$ teaspoon) and two equal parts.

1. LIGHT TONE
Use the first part ($\frac{1}{2}$ teaspoon).
$\frac{1}{8}$ teaspoon Naples Yellow

2. MEDIUM TONE
Use the second part. Leave it as it is.

3. DARK TONE
Use the third part.
Add: $\frac{1}{8}$ teaspoon French Ultramarine
$\frac{1}{8}$ teaspoon purple
$\frac{1}{8}$ teaspoon aqua
smidge Cadmium Orange

4. EXTRA LIGHT TONE
When this is required, to $\frac{1}{2}$ teaspoon light tone.
Add: $\frac{1}{2}$ teaspoon White
smidge Naples Yellow
smidge Cadmium Orange

If the mountains are in the far distance, the dark tone of the sky can be used. This is effective against the extra light sky tone at the horizon.

- For snow-capped mountains mix light and medium tones of white. With your offset knife, paint the light tone where indicated and then paint the medium tone where the shadows appear. Do not cover the mountains entirely with snow as there are usually rocks showing in parts.

Colour mix for rock tones

MEDIUM TONE
¾ teaspoon White
½ teaspoon purple
½ teaspoon Yellow Ochre
smidge mixed green

Mix the paint and separate it into three parts, one small (½ teaspoon) and two equal parts.

1. LIGHT TONE
Use the first part (½ teaspoon).
Add: ½ teaspoon White
¼ teaspoon Naples Yellow
smidge Cadmium Orange

2. MEDIUM TONE
Use the second part. Leave it as it is.

3. DARK TONE
Use the third part.
Add: ¾ teaspoon purple
smidge mixed green

4. EXTRA LIGHT
When this is required, to ½ teaspoon light tone
Add: ½ teaspoon White
smidge Naples Yellow

Mixtures of greyed dark green on page 95 can also be used if desired.

Colour mix for blue tones

MEDIUM TONE
1 teaspoon White
½ teaspoon French Ultramarine
¾ teaspoon aqua
smidge Cadmium Orange

Mix the paint and separate it into three parts, one small (½ teaspoon) and two equal parts.

1. LIGHT TONE
Use the first part (½ teaspoon).
Add: ¼ teaspoon aqua
½ teaspoon White
smidge Naples Yellow

2. MEDIUM TONE
Use the second part. Leave it as it is.

3. DARK TONE
Use the third part.
Add: ¼ teaspoon French Ultramarine
¼ teaspoon aqua
smidge Cadmium Orange

4. EXTRA DARK TONE
When this is required, to ½ teaspoon light tone
Add: ½ teaspoon French Ultramarine

Colour mix for yellow tones

LIGHT

MEDIUM

DARK

EXTRA DARK

MEDIUM TONE

$1\frac{1}{4}$ teaspoons Cadmium Yellow Deep only

Separate the Cadmium Yellow Deep into three parts, one small ($\frac{1}{2}$ teaspoon) and two equal parts.

1. LIGHT TONE

Use the first part ($\frac{1}{2}$ teaspoon).

Add: $\frac{1}{2}$ teaspoon White
$\frac{1}{2}$ teaspoon Lemon Yellow

2. MEDIUM TONE

Use the second part. Leave it as it is.

3. DARK TONE

Use the third part.

Add: $\frac{1}{2}$ teaspoon Yellow Ochre
$\frac{1}{8}$ teaspoon purple

4. EXTRA DARK TONE

When this is required, to $\frac{1}{2}$ teaspoon dark tone

Add: $\frac{1}{2}$ teaspoon Yellow Ochre
$\frac{1}{4}$ teaspoon purple

Alternative tones of yellow

EXTRA LIGHT (LEMON YELLOW)

LIGHT (NAPLES YELLOW)

MEDIUM (CADMIUM YELLOW DEEP)

DARK (YELLOW OCHRE)

The above combination of yellows creates effective tonal values. These tones are useful for painting fruit and flowers. Use the colour straight from the palette unmixed.

Colour mix for red tones

MEDIUM TONE
$1\frac{3}{4}$ teaspoons Vermilion only.

Separate the Vermilion into three parts, one small ($\frac{1}{2}$ teaspoon) and two equal parts.

1. LIGHT TONE
Use the first part ($\frac{1}{2}$ teaspoon).
Add: $\frac{1}{4}$ teaspoon Cadmium Orange
$\frac{3}{4}$ teaspoon White
$\frac{1}{8}$ teaspoon Vermilion

2. MEDIUM TONE
Use the second part. Leave it as it is.

3. DARK TONE
Use the third part.
Add: $\frac{1}{2}$ teaspoon Alizarin Crimson

4. EXTRA DARK TONE
When this is required, to $\frac{1}{2}$ teaspoon dark tone
Add: $\frac{1}{2}$ teaspoon Alizarin Crimson

Alternative tones of red

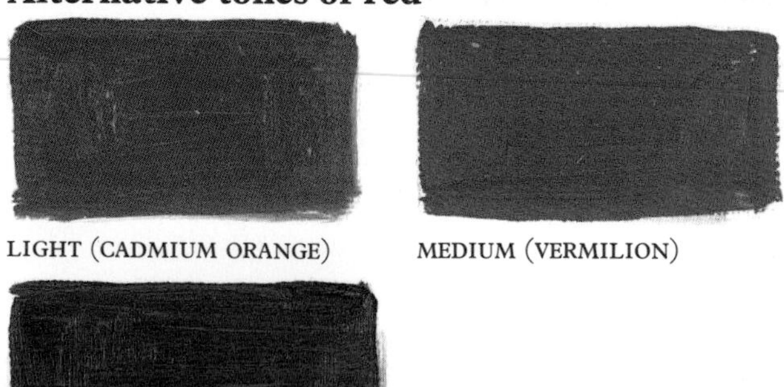

The above combination of reds creates effective tonal values. These tones are useful for painting fruit and flowers. Use the colours straight from the palette unmixed.

Colour mix for orange tones

EXTRA LIGHT

LIGHT

MEDIUM

DARK

MEDIUM TONE
$1\frac{3}{4}$ tablespoons Cadmium Orange only

Separate the Cadmium Orange into three parts, one small ($\frac{1}{2}$ teaspoon) and two equal parts.

1. LIGHT TONE
Use the first part ($\frac{1}{2}$ teaspoon).
Add: $\frac{1}{2}$ teaspoon White
$\frac{1}{4}$ teaspoon Cadmium Yellow Deep

2. MEDIUM TONE
Use the second part. Leave it as it is.

3. DARK TONE
Use the third part.
Add: $\frac{3}{4}$ teaspoon Alizarin Crimson

4. EXTRA LIGHT TONE
When this is required, to $\frac{1}{2}$ teaspoon light tone
Add: $\frac{1}{2}$ teaspoon White
$\frac{1}{8}$ teaspoon Cadmium Yellow Deep

Colour mix for purple tones

LIGHT

MEDIUM

DARK

EXTRA DARK

MEDIUM TONE
1 teaspoon White
$\frac{1}{2}$ teaspoon purple
smidge Yellow Ochre

Mix the paint and separate it into three parts, one small ($\frac{1}{2}$ teaspoon) and two equal parts.

1. LIGHT TONE
Use the first part ($\frac{1}{2}$ teaspoon).
Add: $\frac{1}{2}$ teaspoon White
smidge Naples Yellow

2. MEDIUM TONE
Use the second part. Leave it as it is.

3. DARK TONE
Use the third part.
Add: $\frac{1}{4}$ teaspoon purple
smidge Yellow Ochre
smidge Cadmium Orange

4. EXTRA DARK TONE
When this is required, to $\frac{1}{2}$ teaspoon dark tone.
Add: $\frac{1}{4}$ teaspoon purple
smidge Cadmium Orange

Colour mix for green tones

MEDIUM TONE
$\frac{1}{2}$ teaspoon Yellow Ochre
1 tablespoon mixed green
smidge Vermilion

Mix the paint and separate it into three parts, one small ($\frac{1}{2}$ teaspoon) and two equal parts.

1. LIGHT TONE
Use the first part ($\frac{1}{2}$ teaspoon).
Add: 1 teaspoon White
$\frac{3}{4}$ teaspoon Lemon Yellow

2. MEDIUM TONE
Use the second part. Leave it as it is.

3. DARK TONE
Use the third part.
Add: $\frac{1}{4}$ teaspoon purple
$\frac{1}{4}$ teaspoon mixed green
If the dark tone turns muddy from adding too much purple, add a little extra mixed green.

4. EXTRA LIGHT TONE
When this is required, to $\frac{1}{2}$ teaspoon light tone.
Add: $\frac{1}{2}$ teaspoon White
$\frac{1}{4}$ teaspoon Lemon Yellow

• To create the effect of distance in trees in a painting, take $\frac{1}{2}$ teaspoon each of the light and medium tones of the above green tones and add to each tone $\frac{1}{2}$ teaspoon of light sky tone (see colour mix on page 84).

Colour mix for black tones

DARK TONE
$\frac{1}{2}$ teaspoon Burnt Umber
$\frac{1}{2}$ teaspoon French Ultramarine

Mix the paint and separate it into three parts, one small ($\frac{1}{2}$ teaspoon) and two equal parts.

1. LIGHT TONE
Use the small part ($\frac{1}{4}$ teaspoon).
Add: $\frac{1}{2}$ teaspoon White
tiny smidge Naples Yellow
tiny smidge Cadmium Orange

2. MEDIUM TONE
Use the second part.
Add: $\frac{1}{4}$ teaspoon White
smidge Cadmium Orange

3. DARK TONE
Use the third part. Leave it as it is.

4. EXTRA LIGHT TONE
When this is required, to $\frac{1}{2}$ teaspoon light tone
Add: $\frac{1}{2}$ teaspoon White
smidge Cadmium Orange

Colour mix for white tones

LIGHT

MEDIUM

DARK

EXTRA DARK

LIGHT TONE
$1\frac{3}{4}$ tablespoons White
smidge Naples Yellow (easy does it)

Mix the paint and separate it into three parts.

1. LIGHT TONE
Use the first part. Leave it as it is.

2. MEDIUM TONE
Use the second part.
Add: $\frac{1}{8}$ teaspoon Burnt Umber
smidge aqua
The colour will look beige – if it is too dark, add more white.

3. DARK TONE
Use the third part.
Add: $\frac{1}{8}$ teaspoon Burnt Umber
$\frac{1}{8}$ teaspoon aqua
smidge Cadmium Orange

4. EXTRA DARK TONE
When this is required, to $\frac{1}{2}$ teaspoon dark tone
Add: $\frac{1}{8}$ teaspoon Burnt Umber
smidge Cadmium Orange

GREYED BACKGROUND COLOURS

1. These colours are especially useful in still life as they will not have and should not have the same intensity, vibrance and importance as the subject matter.
2. They can also be used in other objects in painting and are especially important in buildings.
3. If you have a larger canvas and need more background colour, mix another half batch.
4. These colours will look strange on the palette but not on the canvas when the subject is painted in.

Colour mix for greyed tones of burnt orange

EXTRA LIGHT — LIGHT

MEDIUM — DARK

MEDIUM TONE
$1\frac{1}{4}$ teaspoons Cadmium Orange
$\frac{1}{4}$ teaspoon Alizarin Crimson
smidge purple
smidge mixed green (easy does it)

Mix the paint and separate it into three parts, one small ($\frac{1}{2}$ teaspoon) and two equal parts.

1. LIGHT TONE
Use the first part ($\frac{1}{2}$ teaspoon).
Add: $\frac{1}{2}$ teaspoon White
$\frac{1}{4}$ teaspoon Cadmium Yellow Deep

2. MEDIUM TONE
Use the second part. Leave it as it is.

3. DARK TONE
Use the third part.
Add: $\frac{1}{2}$ teaspoon Alizarin Crimson
$\frac{1}{4}$ teaspoon purple
smidge mixed green

4. EXTRA LIGHT TONE
When this is required, to $\frac{1}{2}$ teaspoon light tone
Add: $\frac{1}{2}$ teaspoon White
smidge of Cadmium Yellow Deep

Colour mix for greyed tones of yellow ochre

EXTRA LIGHT LIGHT

MEDIUM DARK

MEDIUM TONE
1 tablespoon Yellow Ochre
$\frac{1}{8}$ teaspoon purple

Mix the paint and separate it into three parts, one small ($\frac{1}{2}$ teaspoon) and two equal parts.

1. LIGHT TONE
Use the first part ($\frac{1}{2}$ teaspoon).
Add: $\frac{1}{2}$ teaspoon White
$\frac{1}{4}$ teaspoon Cadmium Yellow Deep

2. MEDIUM TONE
Use the second part. Leave it as it is.

3. DARK TONE
Use the third part.
Add: $\frac{1}{2}$ teaspoon purple
smidge mixed green

4. EXTRA LIGHT TONE
When this is required, to $\frac{1}{4}$ teaspoon light tone
Add: $\frac{1}{2}$ teaspoon White
smidge Cadmium Yellow Deep

Colour mix for greyed tones of light green

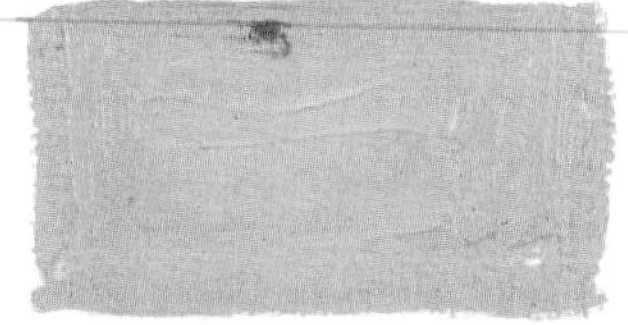

EXTRA LIGHT LIGHT

MEDIUM DARK

MEDIUM TONE
1 tablespoon White
1 teaspoon Yellow Ochre
$\frac{1}{2}$ teaspoon mixed green
smidge purple
smidge Vermilion

Mix the paint and separate it into three parts, one small ($\frac{1}{2}$ teaspoon) and two equal parts.

1. LIGHT TONE
Use the first part ($\frac{1}{2}$ teaspoon).
Add: $\frac{3}{4}$ teaspoon White
smidge Yellow Ochre

2. MEDIUM TONE
Use the second part. Leave it as it is.

3. DARK TONE
Use the third part.
Add: $\frac{1}{4}$ teaspoon purple
smidge mixed green

4. EXTRA LIGHT TONE
When this is required, to $\frac{1}{4}$ teaspoon light tone
Add: $\frac{1}{2}$ teaspoon White

Colour mix for greyed tones of dark green

EXTRA LIGHT LIGHT

MEDIUM DARK

MEDIUM TONE
1 tablespoon Yellow Ochre
¼ teaspoon mixed green
¼ teaspoon Vermilion
¼ teaspoon purple

Mix the paint and separate it into three parts, one small (½ teaspoon) and two equal parts.

1. LIGHT TONE
Use the first part (½ teaspoon).
Add: ½ teaspoon White
smidge Yellow Ochre

2. MEDIUM TONE
Use the second part. Leave it as it is.

3. DARK TONE
Use the third part.
Add: ½ teaspoon purple
⅛ teaspoon Viridian
smidge Yellow Ochre

4. EXTRA LIGHT TONE
When this is required, to ¼ teaspoon light tone
Add: ½ teaspoon White
smidge Yellow Ochre

ALTERNATIVE BACKGROUND COLOURS

These colours are used straight from the palette.

VERMILION PURPLE

ALIZARIN CRIMSON

Paint the background with alternate criss-cross strokes of purple and Alizarin Crimson using the flat of the offset knife. Paint a few criss-cross strokes of Vermilion here and there over the first two background colours – not too much.

MIXTURES FOR COLOUR TINTS

1. These colour tints are invaluable in painting where pastel shades are required.
2. When mixing colours for tints, easy does it as you can always add more.
3. Remember to keep the knife clean when going from one colour to another.

Colour mix for yellow tint

MEDIUM TONE
$1\frac{1}{4}$ teaspoons White
$\frac{1}{2}$ teaspoon Cadmium Yellow Deep
$\frac{1}{8}$ teaspoon Lemon Yellow

Mix the paint and separate it into three parts, one small ($\frac{1}{2}$ teaspoon) and two equal parts.

1. LIGHT TONE
Use the first part ($\frac{1}{2}$ teaspoon).
Add: 1 teaspoon White
$\frac{1}{8}$ teaspoon Lemon Yellow

2. MEDIUM TONE
Use the second part. Leave it as it is.

3. DARK TONE
Use the third part.
Add: $\frac{1}{2}$ teaspoon Cadmium Yellow Deep
$\frac{1}{2}$ teaspoon Yellow Ochre
$\frac{1}{8}$ teaspoon Cadmium Orange

4. EXTRA LIGHT TONE
When this is required, to $\frac{1}{4}$ teaspoon light tone
Add: $\frac{1}{2}$ teaspoon White

Colour mix for orange tint

MEDIUM TONE
1 teaspoon White
$\frac{1}{2}$ teaspoon Cadmium Orange
$\frac{1}{8}$ teaspoon Cadmium Yellow Deep

Mix the paint and separate it into three parts, one small ($\frac{1}{2}$ teaspoon) and two equal parts.

1. LIGHT TONE
Use the first part ($\frac{1}{2}$ teaspoon).
Add: $\frac{3}{4}$ teaspoon White
smidge Cadmium Yellow Deep

2. MEDIUM TONE
Use the second part. Leave it as it is.

3. DARK TONE
Use the third part.
Add: $\frac{3}{4}$ teaspoon Cadmium Orange
smidge Vermilion

4. EXTRA LIGHT TONE
When this is required, to $\frac{1}{4}$ teaspoon light tone
Add: $\frac{1}{2}$ teaspoon White

Colour mix for red tint

EXTRA LIGHT

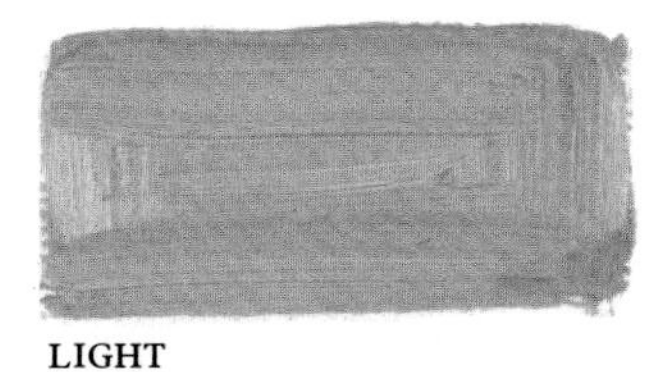

LIGHT

MEDIUM

DARK

MEDIUM TONE
1¼ teaspoons White
½ teaspoon Vermilion
⅛ teaspoon Cadmium Orange

Mix the paint and separate it into three parts, one small (½ teaspoon) and two equal parts.

1. LIGHT TONE
Use the first part (½ teaspoon).
Add: 1 teaspoon White
smidge Naples Yellow
smidge Cadmium Orange

2. MEDIUM TONE
Use the second part. Leave it as it is.

3. DARK TONE
Use the third part.
Add: ¾ teaspoon Vermilion
smidge Cadmium Orange

4. EXTRA LIGHT TONE
When this is required, to ¼ teaspoon light tone
Add: ½ teaspoon white

Colour mix for dark red tint

EXTRA LIGHT

LIGHT

MEDIUM

DARK

MEDIUM TONE
1¼ teaspoons White
½ teaspoon Alizarin Crimson

Mix the paint and separate it into three parts, one small (½ teaspoon) and two equal parts.

1. LIGHT TONE
Use the first part (½ teaspoon).
Add: 1 teaspoon White
smidge Naples Yellow

2. MEDIUM TONE
Use the second part. Leave it as it is.

3. DARK TONE
Use the third part.
Add: ¾ teaspoon Alizarin Crimson
smidge Cadmium Orange

4. EXTRA LIGHT TONE
Add: ½ teaspoon White

Colour mix for lavender purple tint

MEDIUM TONE
$1\frac{1}{2}$ teaspoons White
$\frac{1}{2}$ teaspoon purple
$\frac{1}{4}$ teaspoon Alizarin Crimson

Mix the paint and separate it into three parts, one small ($\frac{1}{2}$ teaspoon) and two equal parts.

1. LIGHT TONE
Use the first part ($\frac{1}{2}$ teaspoon).
Add: 1 teaspoon White
smidge Alizarin Crimson

2. MEDIUM TONE
Use the second part. Leave it as it is.

3. DARK TONE
Use the third part.
Add: $\frac{1}{2}$ teaspoon purple
$\frac{1}{8}$ teaspoon Alizarin Crimson

4. EXTRA LIGHT TONE
When this is required, to $\frac{1}{4}$ teaspoon light tone
Add: $\frac{1}{2}$ teaspoon White

Colour mix for blue purple tint

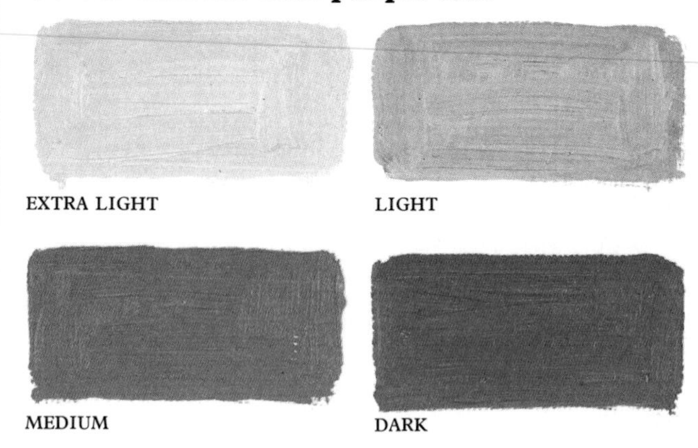

MEDIUM TONE
$1\frac{1}{2}$ teaspoons White
$\frac{1}{2}$ teaspoon purple

Mix the paint and separate it into three parts, one small ($\frac{1}{2}$ teaspoon) and two equal parts.

1. LIGHT TONE
Use the first part ($\frac{1}{2}$ teaspoon).
Add: 1 teaspoon White
smidge Naples Yellow

2. MEDIUM TONE
Use the second part. Leave it as it is.

3. DARK TONE
Use the third part.
Add: $\frac{3}{4}$ teaspoon purple
smidge French Ultramarine

4. EXTRA LIGHT TONE
When this is required, to $\frac{1}{4}$ teaspoon light tone
Add: $\frac{1}{2}$ teaspoon White

Colour mix for blue tint

EXTRA LIGHT

LIGHT

MEDIUM

DARK

MEDIUM TONE
1¼ teaspoons White
¼ teaspoon aqua
⅛ teaspoon French Ultramarine

Mix the paint and separate it into three parts, one small (½ teaspoon) and two equal parts.

1. LIGHT TONE
Use the first part (½ teaspoon).
Add: 1 teaspoon White
smidge aqua

2. MEDIUM TONE
Use the second part for the medium tone. Leave it as it is.

3. DARK TONE
Use the third part.
Add: ¼ teaspoon French Ultramarine
⅛ teaspoon aqua

4. EXTRA LIGHT TONE
When this is required, to ¼ teaspoon light tone
Add: ½ teaspoon White

Colour mix for green tint

EXTRA LIGHT

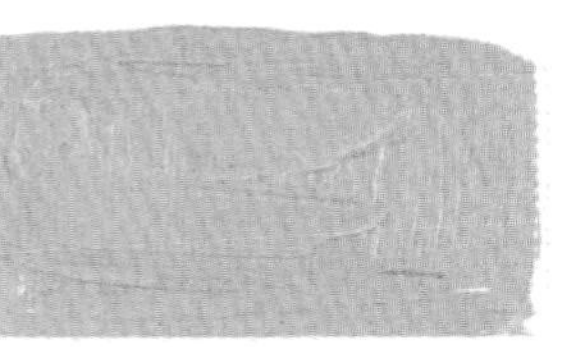

LIGHT

MEDIUM

DARK

MEDIUM TONE
1 teaspoon White
½ teaspoon Yellow Ochre
½ teaspoon mixed green
smidge Cadmium Yellow Deep

Mix the paint and separate it into three parts, one small (½ teaspoon) and two equal parts.

1. LIGHT TONE
Use the first part (½ teaspoon).
Add: 1 teaspoon White
¼ teaspoon Lemon Yellow

2. MEDIUM TONE
Use the second part. Leave it as it is.

3. DARK TONE
Use the third part.
Add: ¼ teaspoon mixed green
smidge purple
smidge Cadmium Yellow Deep

4. EXTRA LIGHT TONE
When this is required, to ¼ teaspoon light tone
Add: ¾ teaspoon White

COLOUR MIXES FOR PORTRAIT PAINTING

Flesh tones are subtle and delicate. Use the darker colours sparingly. You can always add more as you go.

Colour mix for flesh tones

MEDIUM TONE
1 teaspoon White
$\frac{1}{8}$ teaspoon Yellow Ochre
smidge Cadmium Orange
smidge Burnt Umber (easy does it)

Mix the paint and separate it into three parts, one small ($\frac{1}{2}$ teaspoon) and two equal parts.

1. LIGHT TONE
Use the first part ($\frac{1}{2}$ teaspoon).
Add: $\frac{1}{4}$ teaspoon White
smidge Naples Yellow
smidge Cadmium Orange

2. MEDIUM TONE
Use the second part. Leave it as it is.

3. DARK TONE
Use the third part.
Add: smidge Naples Yellow
smidge Cadmium Orange
smidge Burnt Umber (easy does it)
If necessary add more smidges in dark tones. There must be distinct tonal values of light, medium and dark.

4. EXTRA LIGHT TONE (use for highlights)
When this is required, to $\frac{1}{8}$ teaspoon light tone
Add: $\frac{1}{8}$ teaspoon White
smidge Naples Yellow

For painting lips

Remove a bit of the light flesh tone, and keep to one side for using on lips.

1. For lip colour, add a smidge of Vermilion to the light flesh tone.

2. For darker lip tone, for shading, add a smidge of Alizarin Crimson to the light flesh tone.

For painting eyes

1. Dark eyes
Use the dark tone of dark hair for the iris in the centre of the eye, the light tone for the pupil while for the whites of the eyes, use an off-white. To obtain an off-white colour, use the light tone of White plus a tiny smidge of French Ultramarine from the palette. This off-white colour can also be used for the highlight in the centre of the eye.

2. Blue eyes
Use the medium and light tones of blue. The colour mix is on page 88. Use the medium tone for the iris and the light tone for the pupil. Use an off-white for the whites of the eyes. To obtain an off-white colour, use the light tone of White plus a tiny smidge of French Ultramarine from the palette. This off-white colour can also be used for the highlight in the centre of the eye.

For painting hair

The following colour mixes can be used for painting different colours of hair.

1. Light hair

Refer to page 86 for the colour mix of earth tones.

LIGHT *for highlights*

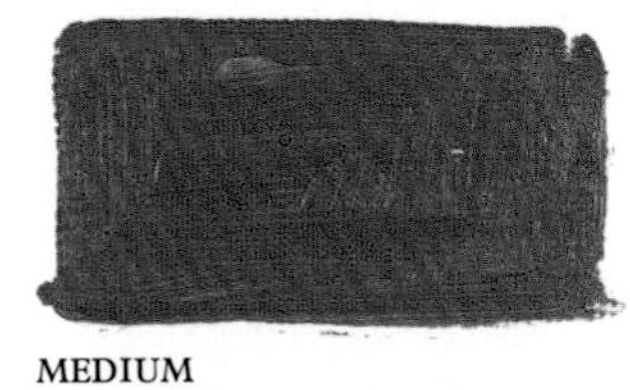

MEDIUM

DARK

EXTRA DARK

Naples Yellow can be used on highlights.

2. Dark hair

Refer to page 87 for the colour mix of tree tones.

LIGHT *for highlights*

MEDIUM

DARK

EXTRA DARK

3. Red hair

Refer to page 93 for the colour mix of greyed background burnt orange.

EXTRA LIGHT *for highlights*

LIGHT

MEDIUM

DARK

4. Grey hair

Refer to page 93 for the colour mix of tones of white.

LIGHT *for highlights*

MEDIUM

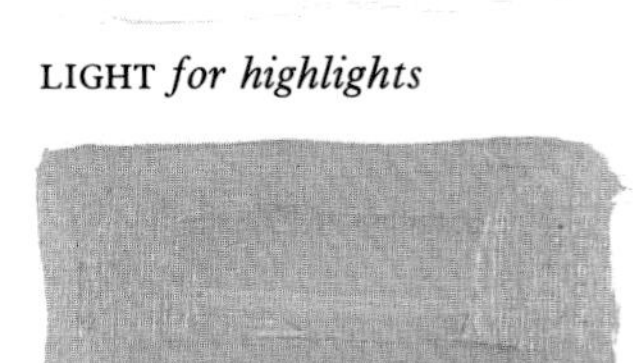

DARK

EXTRA DARK

5. White hair

Use the light, medium and dark tones of white only,

LIGHT

MEDIUM

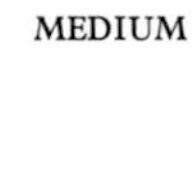

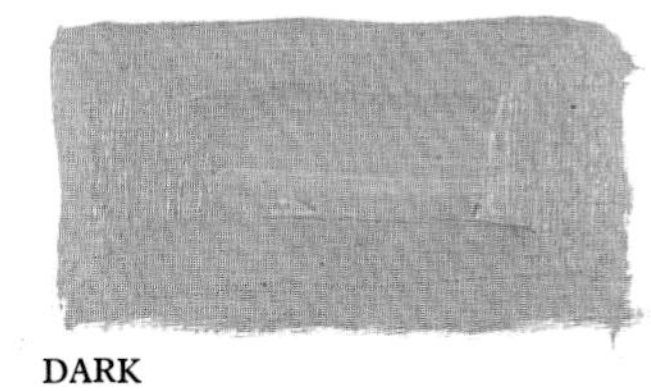

DARK

Paintings to practise

Use a canvas 14 by 18 inches (36 by 46 cm). Study the drawings on pages 102, 104, 105, and also the finished painting. Then proceed as follows:

1. Cover the canvas with an umber wash. To make the umber wash, squeeze out $\frac{1}{2}$ teaspoonful of Burnt Umber. Dip the large, flat, bristle brush into the turpentine – make sure that it is not dripping too much – and then dip the brush into the Burnt Umber on the palette, pulling some aside to make a light, rather thin wash. Cover the canvas with the umber wash, taking care not to make the canvas too dark or runny. Wipe off any excess moisture with toilet tissue but leave the canvas damp.

2. To divide the canvas up into sections, use the medium, round brush and umber wash. Use slightly more Burnt Umber than turpentine in order to achieve a darker colour wash than before. The canvas is to be used horizontally in this painting, so draw three horizontal lines equally spaced and five vertical lines, also equally spaced. A useful tip is to divide the canvas into quarters first. The sections do not have to be measured off exactly. See the drawing below.

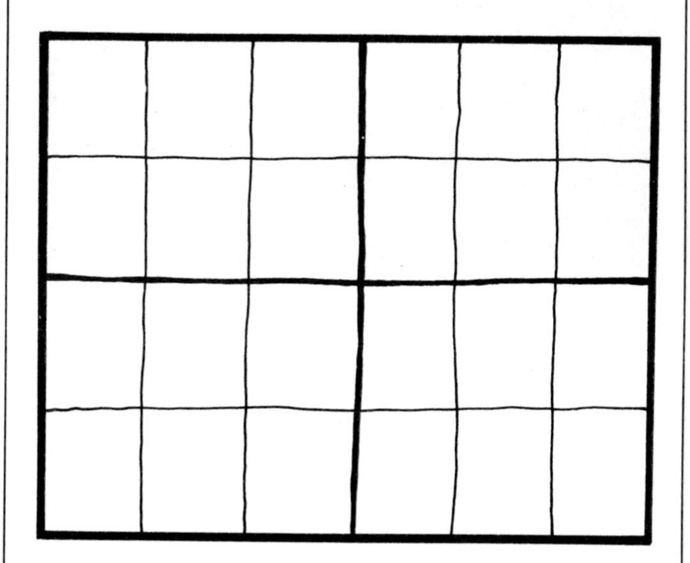

The finished painting

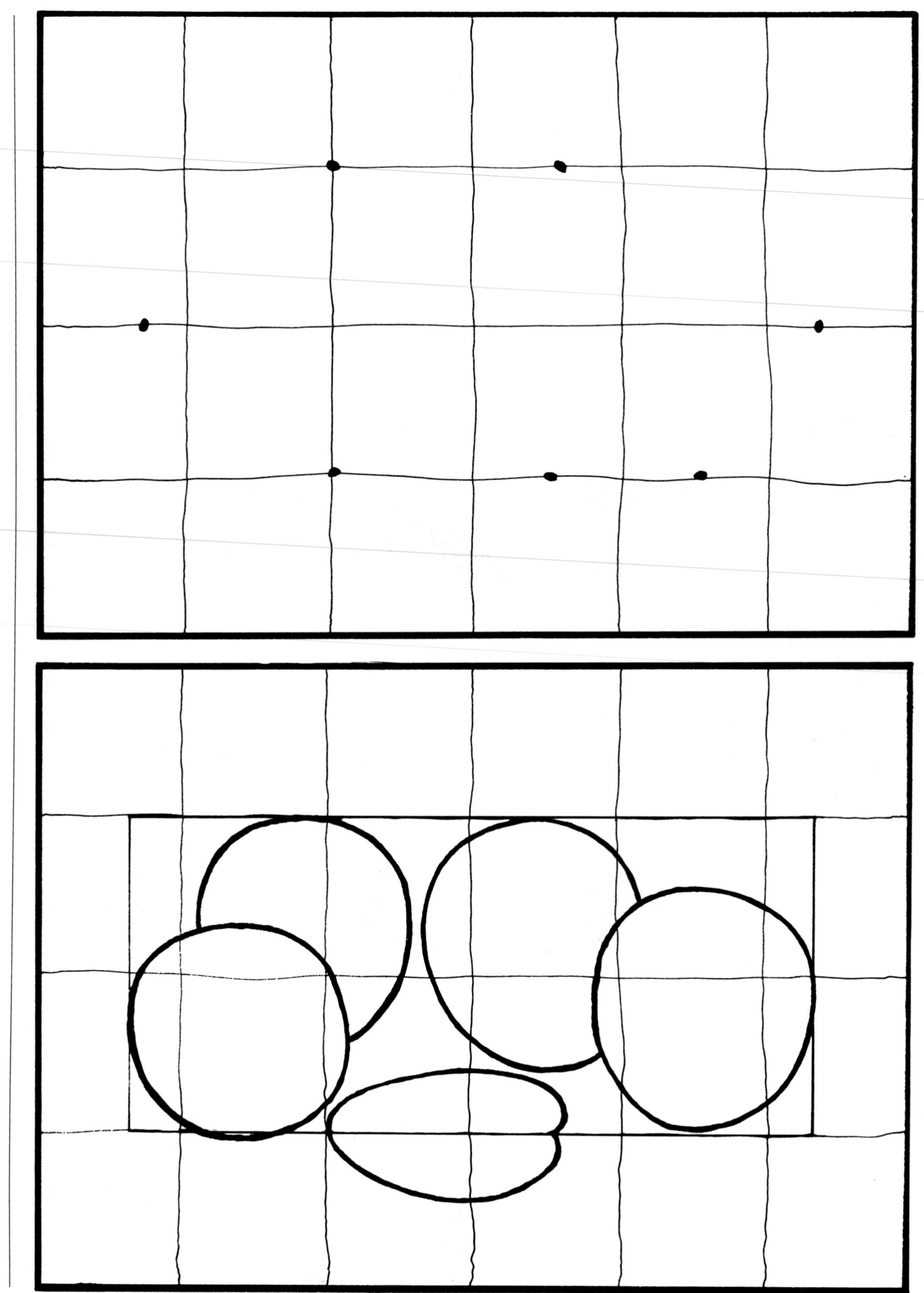

3. To help with placing work on the canvas, use the squares as guidelines and draw in the dots as shown in the drawing opposite above, using the darker umber wash.

4. Draw in circles for the apples and a half circle for the cut apple, using the drawing opposite below and the finished painting as a guideline.

5. In this painting, the light is coming from the right. Lightly put in the shadows as in the drawing above.

6. The colour mixes to use are shown in the drawing below. Remember to use round strokes when painting the apples to keep the form. The colour mix of greyed dark green is used for the background. Use purple for the tips of the stems.

7. Refer to the index at the end of the book for the colour mixes needed.

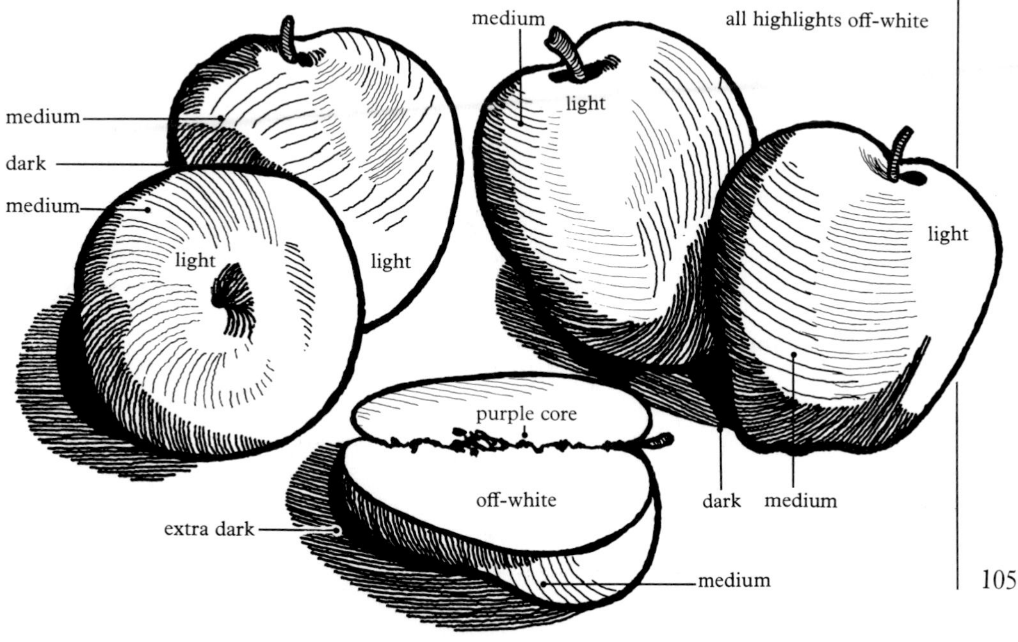

PEARS

Use a canvas 9 by 12 inches (23 by 30 cm). Study the drawings on this page and also the finished painting. Then proceed as follows:

1. Cover the canvas with an umber wash. To make the umber wash, squeeze out $\frac{1}{2}$ teaspoonful of Burnt Umber. Dip the large, flat, bristle brush into the turpentine – make sure that it's not dripping too much – and then dip the brush into the Burnt Umber on the palette, pulling some aside to make a light, rather thin wash. Cover the canvas with the wash, taking care not to make it too dark or runny. Wipe off any excess moisture with toilet tissue but leave the canvas damp.

2. To divide the canvas up into sections, use the medium, round brush and umber wash. This time, use slightly more Burnt Umber than turpentine in order to achieve a darker colour wash than before. The canvas is to be used horizontally in this painting, so draw three horizontal lines equally spaced and five vertical lines, also equally spaced. A useful tip is to divide the canvas into quarters first. The sections do not have to be measured off exactly. See the drawing below.

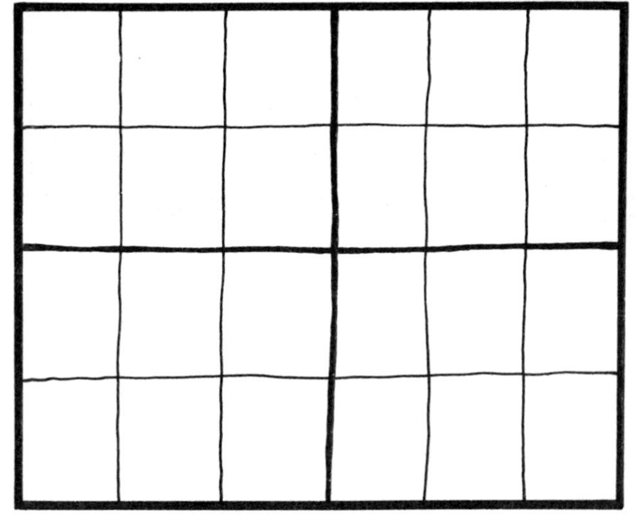

3. To help with placing work on the canvas, use the squares as guidelines and draw in the dots as shown in the drawing below.

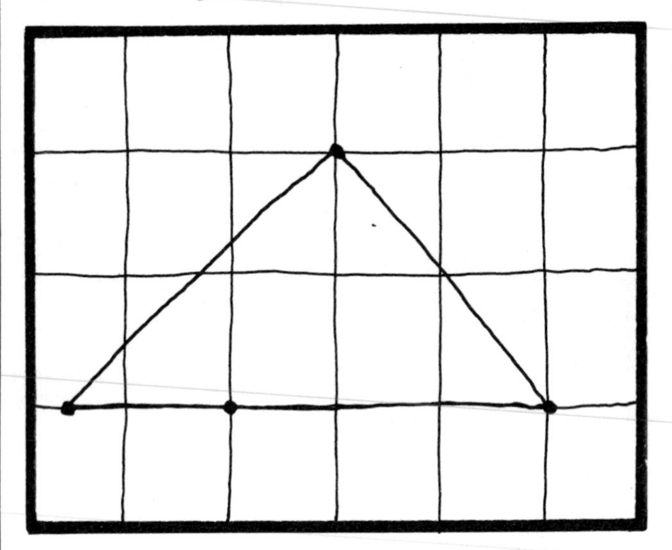

4. Study the drawing below and note that the light is coming from the right, therefore the shadows are on the left. Refer to the index for the colour mixes required.

5. Use the greyed dark green colour mix for the background. Paint the background first before you start on the fruit.

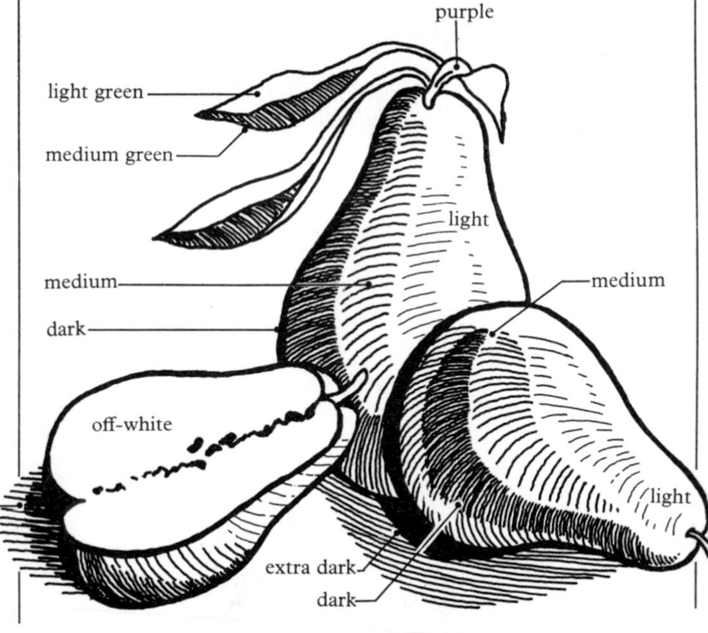

The finished painting

ORANGES

Use a canvas 9 by 12 inches (23 by 30 cm). Study the drawings on this page and also the finished painting. Then proceed as follows:

1. Cover the canvas with an umber wash. To make the umber wash, squeeze out $\frac{1}{2}$ teaspoonful of Burnt Umber. Dip the large, flat, bristle brush into the turpentine – make sure that it's not dripping too much – and then into the Burnt Umber on the palette, pulling some aside with the brush to make a light, rather thin wash. Cover the canvas with the wash, taking care not to make it too dark or runny. Wipe off any excess moisture with toilet tissue but leave the canvas damp.

2. To divide the canvas up into sections, use the medium, round brush and umber wash. This time, use slightly more Burnt Umber than turpentine in order to achieve a darker colour wash than before. The canvas is to be used horizontally in this painting, so draw three horizontal lines equally spaced across the canvas and five vertical lines, also equally spaced. A useful tip is to divide the canvas into quarters first. The sections do not have to be measured off exactly. See the drawing below.

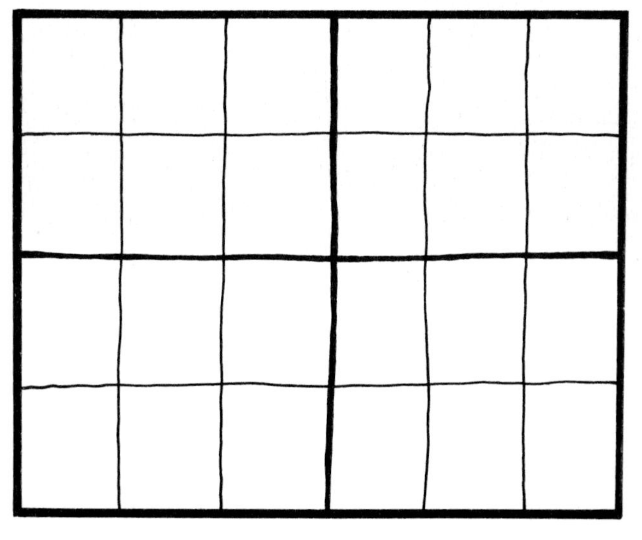

3. To help with placing work on the canvas, use the squares as guidelines and draw in the dots as shown in the drawing below.

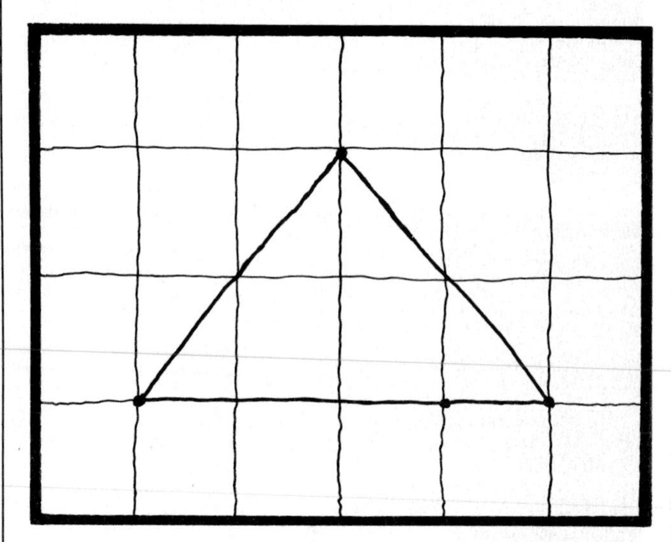

4. Study the drawing below and note that the light is coming from the right, therefore the shadows are on the left. Refer to the index at the end of the book for the colour mixes required.

5. Use the greyed dark green colour mix for the background. Paint the background before you start on the fruit.

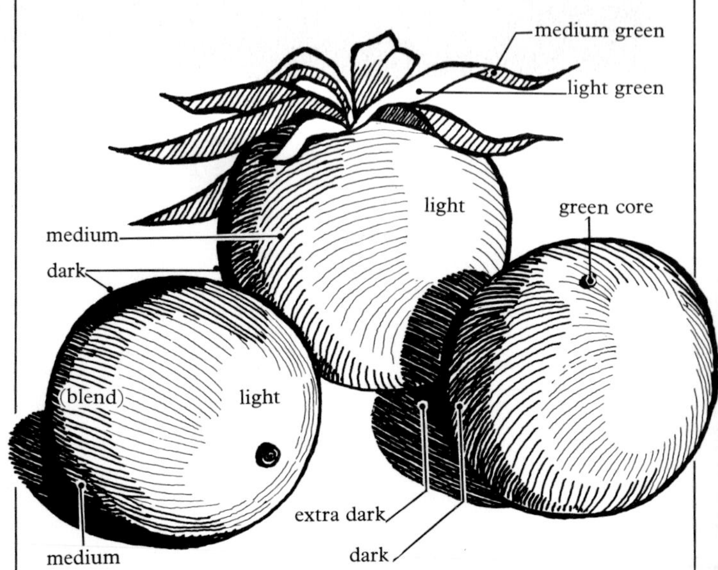

The finished painting

SPRING BOUQUET

Still life is better for a beginner: it is less demanding and much more rewarding. I have chosen this wild spring bouquet for you to practise mixing the colour tints. If you have any mixed colours left over you can keep the paint (see page 117) to use on other small flower paintings. Look at the drawing and the finished painting carefully.

The drawing

1. Use a canvas 14 by 18 inches (36 by 46 cm). You may use a smaller or larger canvas as long as it has the same proportion to place the subject correctly. The smaller size will, of course, save on the amount of paint required.

2. Arrange the palette according to the instructions on page 78.

3. Using the large, flat, hog bristle brush, stain the canvas with a light wash of Burnt Umber as described on page 75. Wipe off the surplus wash with toilet tissue but still leave the canvas damp.

4. With the medium, round brush and dark umber wash, draw in the grid lines and the simple drawing.

5. In this picture, the light is coming from the left – note the highlights on the petals – so lightly shade the flowers where indicated.

6. Clean the brushes you have used so far in turpentine, using some toilet tissue.

The painting

The background is painted in first.

1. Refer to page 95 for the colour mixes for greyed dark green and mix the paint according to the instructions.

2. Using the offset knife, paint the dark greyed green tone on the right of the canvas, then the medium tone, and the light and extra light tone on the left. Remember to blend the tones slightly into one another for depth. Clean the knife.

Flowers

1. Because the painting is a multi-coloured floral, it is logical when you mix one colour to paint all the flowers in that one colour at the same time before going on to a second colour. Study the painting carefully.

2. The flower drawings I have drawn for you here are precise so that you can understand the structure and colour area. You will notice that the finished painting is much more impressionistic. Try for a looser painting yourself. It is more important to retain tonal values than form. Practise painting a few flowers before going to canvas.

Orange flowers

Use the colour mix for the orange tint on page 96.

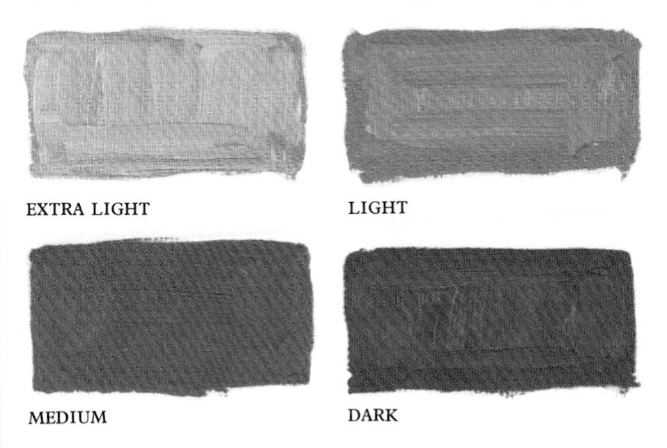

1. Mix the paint according to the instructions.

2. Paint all the orange flowers, beginning with the dark tone, then continuing with the medium, light and extra light tones. Keep any leftover paint. Do not paint any of the tones over one another. This will muddy and destroy the tonal values. Only blend the tones where they meet. Keep the strokes free and easy.

3. Paint the centres of the flowers last. All the flowers have the same colour centre. Use Yellow Ochre straight from the palette. Paint the centres with round strokes. Finally, apply a highlight of Naples Yellow from the palette to the centre.

4. Clean the knife before painting another colour.

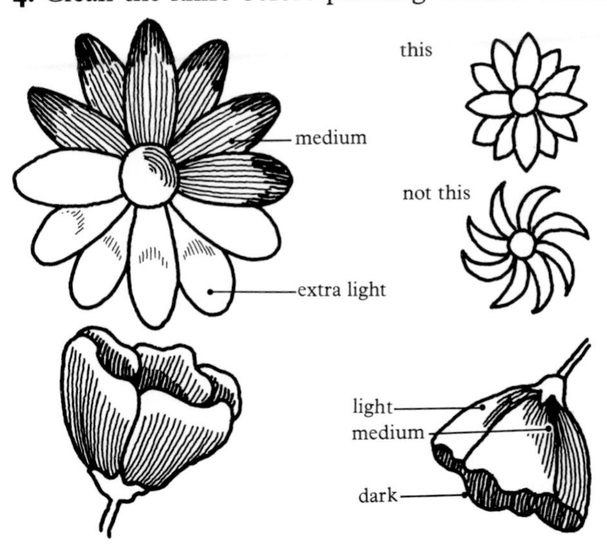

Pink flowers
Use the colour mix for the red tint on page 97.

1. Mix the paint according to the instructions.

2. Paint all the pink flowers starting with the dark tone, then continue with the medium, light and extra light tones. Keep any leftover paint. Do not paint any of the tones over one another. This will muddy and destroy the tonal values. Only blend the tones where they meet.

3. Paint the centres of the flowers last, using Yellow Ochre straight from the palette. Paint the centres with round strokes. Finally, apply a highlight of Naples Yellow from the palette to the centre.
4. Clean the knife before painting another colour.

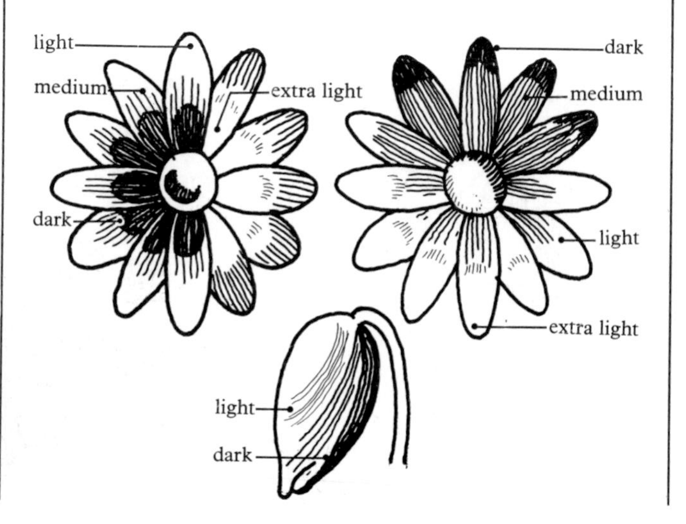

Yellow flowers
Use the colour mix for the yellow tint on page 96.

1. Mix the paint according to the instructions.

2. Paint all the yellow flowers, starting with the dark tone, then continue with the medium, light and extra light tones. Keep any leftover paint. Do not paint any of the tones over one another. This will muddy and destroy the tonal values. Only blend the tones where they meet at the edges.

3. Put a wavy line of Vermilion between the light and medium colours (see drawing below).

4. Paint the centres of the flowers last, using Yellow Ochre straight from the palette. Paint the centres with round strokes. Finally, apply a highlight of Naples Yellow from the palette to the centre.

5. Clean the knife before painting another colour.

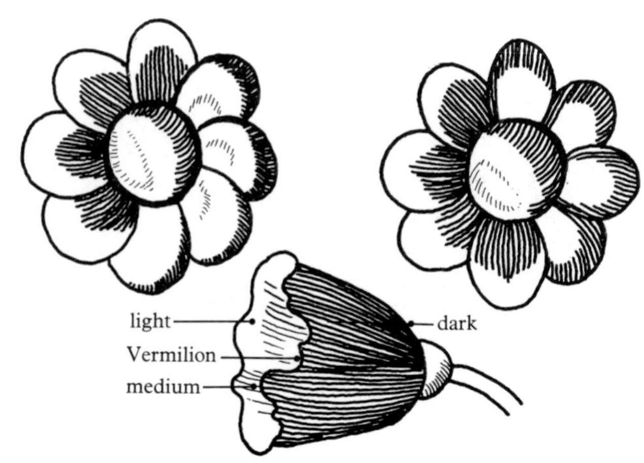

Purple flowers

Use the mix for the lavender purple tint on page 98.

1. Mix the paint according to the instructions.

2. Paint all the purple flowers, starting with the dark tone, and continuing with the medium, light and extra light tones. Remember to keep the tonal values. Keep any leftover paint.

3. Referring to the drawings, paint the centre of one flower as usual, using Yellow Ochre straight from the palette. For the second and third flowers take some purple straight from the palette and paint a wavy line between the dark and medium areas on the flowers.

4. Paint the centres of the rest of the purple flowers as usual, using Yellow Ochre straight from the palette. Paint the centres with round strokes. Finally, apply a highlight of Naples Yellow from the palette to the centre of the flowers.

5. Clean the knife before painting another colour.

White flowers

Use the colour mix for tones of white on page 93.

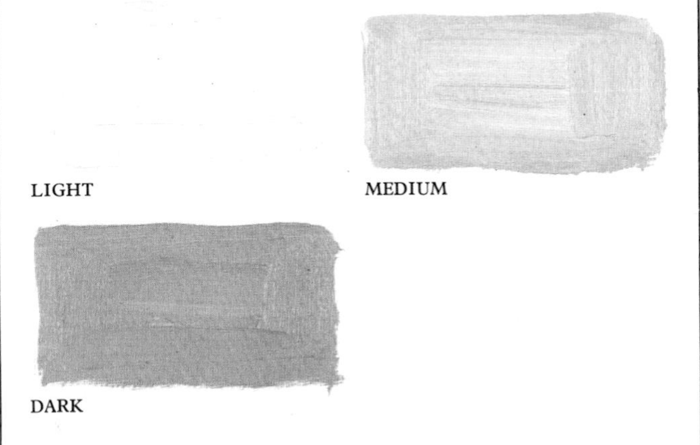

1. Mix the paint according to the instructions, remembering not to make up the extra dark tone of white.

2. Paint the small flowers in two tones only, the light and medium tones. Paint the yellow centres of the flowers, using Yellow Ochre straight from the palette. Paint the buds in the same tones, remembering to keep them looking delicate.

3. Paint all the other white flowers with the dark, medium and light tones. Keep any leftover paint.

4. Paint the centres of the rest of the white flowers last, using Yellow Ochre straight from the palette. Paint the centres with round strokes. Finally, apply a highlight of Naples Yellow from the palette to the centre of the flowers.

5. Clean the knife before painting another colour.

Blue flowers

Use the colour mix for the blue tint on page 99.

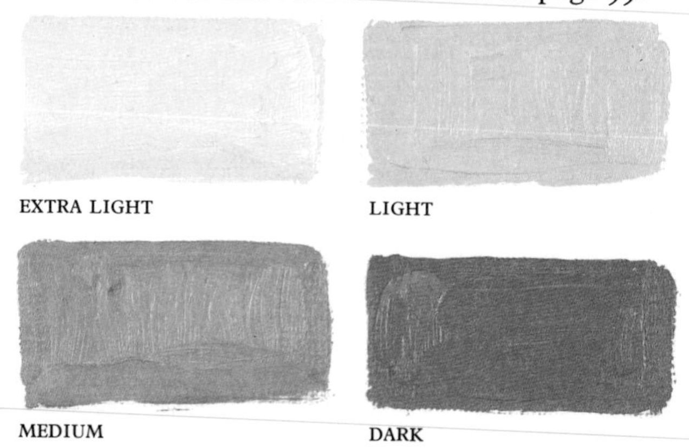

1. Mix the paint according to the instructions.

2. Paint the large blue flowers, using the dark, medium, light and extra light tones.

3. Paint the small blue flowers in dark and extra light tones only. Keep the flowers delicate.

4. Paint the centres of the flowers last, using Yellow Ochre straight from the palette. Apply the paint to the centres with round strokes. Finally, apply a highlight of Naples Yellow from the palette to the centre.

5. Clean the knife before painting another colour.

6. The ribbon will be painted in the same blue tones later on, so keep any leftover paint carefully.

Leaves and stems

Use the colour mix of tones of green on page 92.

1. Study the drawing and painting on pages 48 and 49. Remember to paint only impressions of leaves, using the different tonal values of green.

2. Mix the paint according to the instructions.

3. Paint the stems at the bottom with dark and medium tones on the right hand side of the canvas and with light and extra light tones on the left hand side of the canvas.

4. On the left hand side of the painting, between the flowers, and on the background, paint in impressions of light and extra light tones of green leaves – don't paint in too many.

5. Paint dark and medium tones of green leaves on the righthand side and the dark side and in between the flowers – don't paint in too many. Keep the leaves indistinct.

6. Clean the knife before painting in the ribbon.

Ribbon

1. Finally, paint the ribbon on the stems, using the dark and light and extra light blue tones – keep the ribbon delicate and flowing.

2. Put any leftover piles of paint neatly onto a tin foil dish, cover with cling film and put the dish in the freezer for use on smaller canvases.

COLOUR COMBINATIONS FOR OTHER FLORAL PAINTINGS

If you have leftover paint, you can have fun mixing and matching the paints for other floral paintings. Use small 9 by 12 inch (23 by 30 cm) canvases. Here are some suggestions for colour schemes to use. Try these combinations or make up your own.

1.

Background: tones of yellow	page 89
Flowers: tones of white	page 93

2.

Background: tones of light greyed green	page 94
Flowers: orange tint	page 96
Daisies: yellow tint	page 96

3.

Background: dark greyed green	page 95
Flowers: red tint	page 97
Small flowers: tones of white	page 93

4.

Background: greyed yellow ochre	page 94
Flowers: blue tint	page 99
Flowers: yellow tint	page 96

5.

Background: light greyed green	page 94
Flowers: blue purple tint	page 98
Flowers: yellow tint	page 96

Leaves and stems of all flowers: tones of green	page 92

LANDSCAPE – REFLECTIONS

This landscape exercise is primarily for you to learn how to refer to the index of colour formulas and how to mix colour and to paint on your own. Don't panic – you will be very pleased and surprised at your first efforts. In this painting you will be learning how to paint water and snow-capped mountains. Look at the drawing and finished painting carefully.

The drawing

1. Use a canvas 14 by 18 inches (36 by 46 cm).

2. Arrange the palette according to the instructions on page 78.

3. Using the large, flat hog bristle brush, stain the canvas with a light wash of Burnt Umber as described on page 75. Wipe off any surplus wash with toilet tissue but leave the canvas damp.

4. With the medium round brush and dark umber wash, draw in the grid lines (see page 75) and simple drawing (see opposite).

5. In this painting the light is coming from the right. Note the light on the righthand side of the mountains, trees and water.

The sky

This is always painted in first. Use the offset knife for painting. Paint the extra light tone along the top of the mountains, continuing with the other tones. Remember to blend the paint where the tones meet.

The mountains

Paint the mountains before adding the snow. Keep the mountains darker at the base. Watch the shape of the strokes. Use the drawing below as a guideline.

How to create the effect of mountains using the flat of the offset knife

Snow

Mix the light and medium tones of white only. Paint snow only where indicated on the finished painting. Not too much!

The hills

Add purple to the dark green tone of the hills where indicated. Paint some green tones for the strip of land running from the trees.

The lake

Paint all the water tones separately and only blend them where they meet for sharp reflections. Paint green tones in the water for reflection of the hills and trees. Run strokes through the water from left to right with the clean tip of the knife. Keep on cleaning the knife as you do this. This will give the water a 'wet' look.

The trees

Keep them slender and tall, and uneven in height. Paint purple at the base of the trees and use it for the shadows of the trees on the ground.

Now that you have finished this painting all on your own, you have probably been encouraged to try painting your own subjects. Keep on painting!

LANDSCAPE – FIELD OF POPPIES

How to paint from a picture postcard or a photograph using the colour mixes in the book.

1. The above postcard is a simple composition. Later on you can copy from your own postcards.

2. Cover the postcard with cling film if you do not want to mark it. Draw grids as illustrated with a round brush and Burnt Umber wash. To make the umber wash, squeeze out $\frac{1}{2}$ teaspoonful of Burnt Umber. Dip the brush into the turpentine – it should not be dripping – and then into the Burnt Umber on the palette, pulling some aside to make a light, rather thin wash. To draw the grids on a horizontal photograph, draw three horizontal lines equally spaced and five vertical lines, also equally spaced. A useful tip is to divide the photograph up into quarters first, then divide each section as indicated. The sections do not have to be measured and exact.

3. Using the grids on the photograph as a guide, it is now easy to proceed with the real canvas.

4. Use a 14 by 18 inch (36 by 46 cm) canvas which has been stained with an umber wash as described on page 75.

5. Using the same umber wash as that used on the photograph – make sure that this umber wash is slightly darker than that used for staining the canvas by using more Burnt Umber than turpentine – divide the canvas up into sections using the same method.

6. Decide where the light is coming from and shade in the drawing as indicated. In this photograph the light is coming from the right. Notice the shadows under the trees and in the foreground.

The sky

This is always painted in first. Use the colour mix for sky tones on page 84.

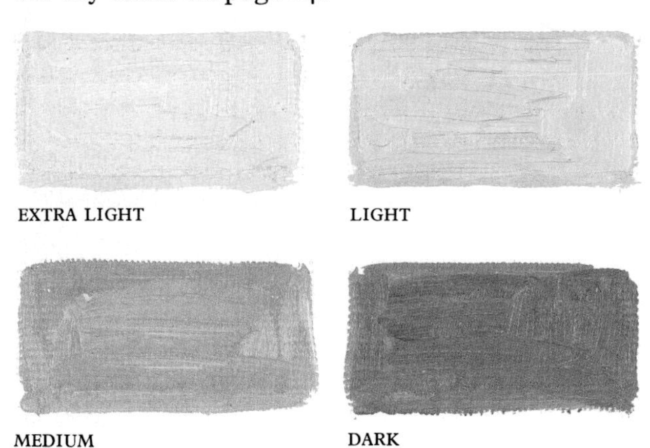

1. Mix the paint according to the instructions.

2. With the offset knife, paint the extra light sky tone along the top of the hills in the distance. Continue with the light tone above it and then the medium tone at the top of the canvas. Blend the tones lightly.

3. Paint the lefthand side of the hills with the dark sky tone and the medium sky tone on the righthand side. Blend slightly. Keep the hills soft and rounded. When the hills or mountains are at a great distance, the third tone of the sky is used and painted in with the sky at the same time.

The field

Use the colour mix for tones of green on page 92.

1. Mix the paint according to the instructions.

2. Paint the dark green tone on the lefthand side of the field, followed by the medium, light and extra light tones as you move towards the righthand side of the canvas. Keep the paint textured and uneven. Remember that the field is not a lawn. Blend the tones of green slightly.

3. Paint the dark green tone with the purple along the front of the field as indicated, giving the appearance of weeds and wild flowers. Use touches of blue and white for this.

4. Paint the dark green tone with purple under the trees for the shadows.

The trees

1. Study the trees in the painting on page 123.

2. The tree trunks in this painting will be painted in purple used straight from the palette.

3. Use the tones of green previously mixed for the field.

4. Paint in the small trees in the background, on the righthand side of the canvas, in the dark green tone on the lefthand side of the trees and in the medium tone on the righthand side. Use short strokes. Scratch the tree trunks unevenly with a knife when the paint is still wet.

5. Paint the tree trunks of the trees on the left unevenly spaced and not like little soldiers! Draw in the branches.

6. Paint the dark green of the foliage first, then the medium tone and the light tone on top of the mass. Keep the tones separated as shown in the painting. Keep the foliage uneven and loose.

7. Paint a little purple near the trunk on the foliage.

The houses

Paint these very small. Use the colour mixes for the extra light, medium and dark sky tones on page 84.

EXTRA LIGHT

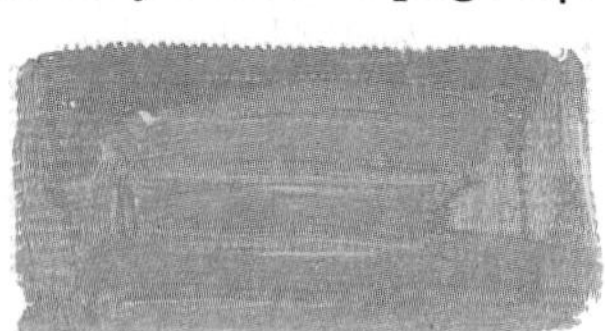

MEDIUM

DARK

1. Paint a bit of the extra light sky tone on the front of the houses, and the medium tone on the side as indicated in the finished painting.

2. Paint the roof tops in Vermilion, which has been mixed with a bit of the dark sky tone.

Winter

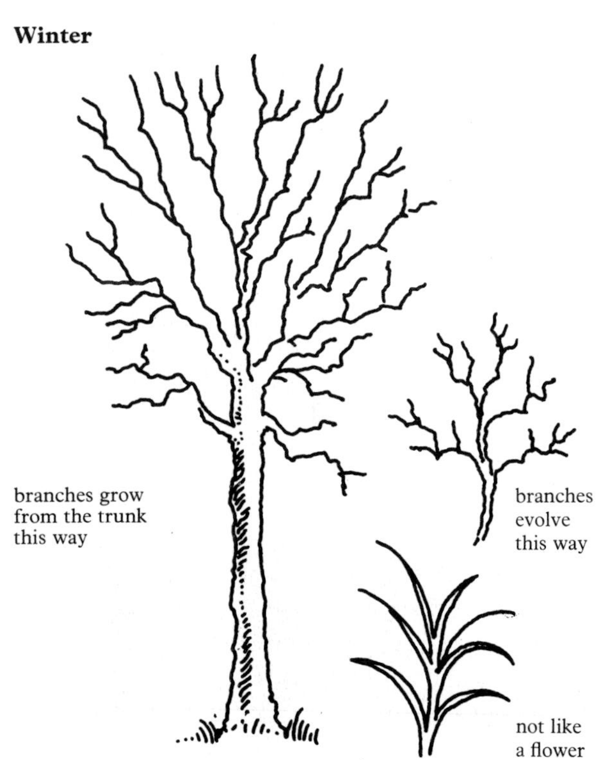

Summer

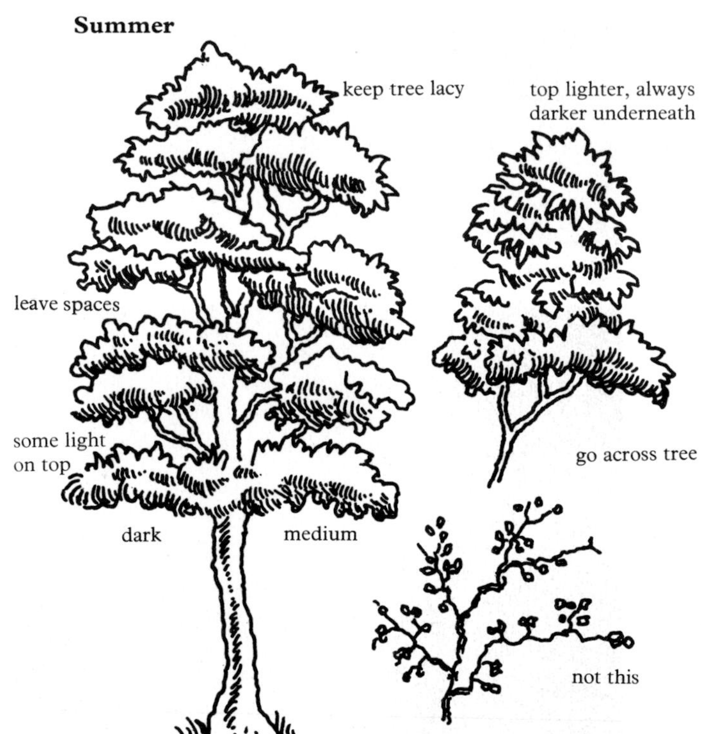

The poppies

Use the three tones of red straight from the palette without any mixing.

LIGHT (CADMIUM ORANGE)

DARK (ALIZARIN CRIMSON)

MEDIUM (VERMILION)

1. Paint tiny orange blobs of poppies on the right or light side of the field where indicated. Keep the poppies uneven and do not paint them in too thickly. Paint some Alizarin Crimson poppies here and there.

2. Paint Vermilion here and there underneath the orange blobs for shadows. Not too many!

3. Paint Vermilion blobs on the lefthand side of the field, with Alizarin Crimson blobs underneath for shadows.

4. Paint a few orange blobs here and there in the darker section of the poppies.

5. Remember to show the green of the field between the mass of poppies.